Acclaim for Edwidge Danticat's **BROTHER, I'M DYING**

"Taut, autobiographical and admirably reported. . . . If *Brother, I'm Dying* does not break your heart, you don't have one. It is not often that, a day after closing a book, one writes a review interrupted by tears, by lumps in the throat. Such are the aftershocks of the story Danticat tells." —*The Philadelphia Inquirer*

"Elegiac. . . . [A] delicate and thoughtful memoir of family and grief." —*Entertainment Weekly*

"In telling her family's story [Danticat] gives us a memoir whose clear-eyed prose and unflinching adherence to the facts conceal an astringent undercurrent of melancholy, a mixture of homesickness and homelessness. Haunting the book throughout is a fear of missed chances, long-overdue payoffs and family secrets withering on the vine: a familiar anxiety when one generation passes to another too quickly." —*The New York Times Book Review*

"*Brother, I'm Dying* gracefully moves in and out of time, mixing past and present experiences. This is a supple, elegant book that ends with both joy and heartbreak." —*USA Today*

"Stunning. . . . Danticat has written a moving tribute to her father and uncle, the two men who raised her. . . . A beautiful memoir to both her fathers." —*The Christian Science Monitor*

Edwidge Danticat

BROTHER, I'M DYING

Edwidge Danticat is the author of numerous books, including *Breath, Eyes, Memory*; *Krik? Krak!*, a National Book Award finalist; *The Farming of Bones*, an American Book Award winner; and *The Dew Breaker*, a PEN/Faulkner Award finalist and winner of the first Story Prize. She lives in Miami with her husband and daughter.

Edwidge Danticat is available for lectures and readings. For information regarding her availability, please visit www.knopfspeakersbureau.com or call 212-572-2013.

BROTHER, I'M DYING

BROTHER, I'M DYING

Edwidge Danticat

Vintage Books
A Division of Random House, Inc.
New York

FIRST VINTAGE BOOKS EDITION, SEPTEMBER 2008

Portions of this book have appeared in slightly different form in *Boston Haitian Reporter*,
The Nation, and O, *The Oprah Magazine*.

Brother, I'm Dying is a work of nonfiction, but the names of certain individuals, as well as
potentially identifying descriptive details concerning them, have been changed.

The Library of Congress has cataloged the Knopf edition as follows:
Danticat, Edwidge.
Brother I'm dying / by Edwidge Danticat.—1st ed.
p. cm.
1. Danticat, Edwidge—Family. 2. Authors, American—20th century—Biography.
3. Uncles—Haiti. 4. Emigration and immigration. 5. Haiti—Social conditions—
20th century. I. Title.
PS3554.A5815Z46 2007
813'.54—dc22 [B] 2007006887

Vintage ISBN: 978-1-4000-3430-7

Book design by Iris Weinstein

www.vintagebooks.com

Printed in the United States of America
20 19 18 17

For the next generation of "cats":
Nadira, Ezekiel,
Zora, Timothy
and Mira

To begin with death. To work my way back into life,
and then, finally, to return to death.
Or else: the vanity of trying to say anything about anyone.

PAUL AUSTER,
The Invention of Solitude

Contents

CONTENTS

PART ONE

HE IS MY BROTHER

This is how you can show your love to me:
Everywhere we go, say of me, "He is my brother."

GENESIS 20:13

Have You Enjoyed Your Life?

I found out I was pregnant the same day that my father's rapid weight loss and chronic shortness of breath were positively diagnosed as end-stage pulmonary fibrosis.

It was a hot morning in early July 2004. I took a six thirty a.m. flight from Miami to accompany my father on a visit to a pulmonologist at Brooklyn's Coney Island Hospital that afternoon. I'd planned to catch up on my sleep during the flight, but cramping in my lower abdomen kept me awake.

I interpreted the cramps as a sign of worry for my father. In the past few months his breathing had grown labored and loud and he'd been hospitalized three times. During his most recent hospital stay, he had been referred to a pulmonologist, who'd since performed a new battery of tests.

My father picked me up at the airport at nine a.m. We hadn't seen each other in a month. Two years before, in August 2002, I had married and moved to Miami, where my then fiancé was living. Fearing my father's disapproval, I hadn't announced my intention to leave New York until a month before the wedding when my father summoned me to his room for a chat.

"How can you leave New York?" he asked while filling out a check on top of a book on his lap. Back then he was still healthy, yet lanky, with a body that looked and moved like an aging dancer's, a receding hairline and half a head of salt-and-pepper hair.

Removing his steel-rimmed bifocals so I could better see his amber eyes, he had added in his slow, scratchy voice, "Your mother's here in Brooklyn. I'm here. Two of your three brothers are here. You have no family in Miami. What if this man you're moving there for mistreats you? Who are you going to turn to?"

The lecture ended with his handing me the equivalent of five months of his mortgage payments toward the wedding reception costs. Looking back now, I wish he'd simply said, "Don't go. I'm going to get sick and I might die."

At the airport, my father was too weak to get out of the car to greet me.

The blistering heat made his breathing even more diffi-cult, he explained on his cell phone, while waving from the driver's seat of his apple red Lincoln Town Car, a car he used as both a gypsy cab and a family car.

When he leaned over to open the door, he began to cough, a deep and hollow cough that produced a mouthful of thick phlegm, which he spat out in paper napkins piled up in a plastic bag next to him.

During the six months that he'd been visibly sick, my father had grown ashamed of this cough, just as he'd been embarrassed about his arms and legs over the many years he'd battled chronic psoriasis and eczema. Then too he'd felt like a "biblical leper," the kind people feared might infect them with skin-ravaging microbes and other ills. So whenever he coughed, he covered his entire face with both his hands.

I waited for him to stop coughing, then leaned over and kissed him. The blunt edge of his high cheekbones struck my lips hard. He had taken to wearing a jacket even on the warmest days because he wanted to hide how much thinner he'd become. That morning at the airport he wore a gray sweater, a striped blue shirt and navy pants that looked like they belonged to someone twice his size.

"I'm happy to see you," he said while tugging at his too wide shirt collar.

Merging into traffic at the airport exit, he asked about my husband and the house we'd been renovating in the Little Haiti section of Miami for the past two years.

"Any new developments?" he winked. "Baby?"

Fedo, my husband, and I were waiting to complete the renovations before trying to get pregnant, I told him.

"You're thirty-five years old," he said. "You have more childbearing years behind you than you do ahead."

Watching him effortlessly drive the same car he'd been driving for nearly a decade, I felt my stomach cramp again. We had a few hours still before his doctor's appointment, so he suggested we visit an herbalist that his pastor, a minister whose Pentecostal church my father had been attending for more than thirty years, had recently recommended.

"Maybe the herbalist can examine us both," I suggested. At that point, I still wanted to believe that our discomforts might be comparable, something that a few herbs and aromatic plants could fix.

The herbalist saw us immediately even though we didn't have an appointment. A large Jamaican woman with a knit rainbow head wrap, she motioned my father to a chair next to a machine that looked like it was set up for an eye exam.

Before our iridology scans, she made us sign disclaimers saying we knew she wasn't a medical doctor and could not cure any illness. This, she explained, was a legal necessity even though she had healed many people—as my father's pastor had told him—including some terminal cancer patients.

She snapped a picture of each of my father's pupils, then enlarged them on a computer screen. Leaning in, she examined the whites of his eyes on the screen.

"You need plenty of vitamins." She pointed out some tiny spots to prove it. "You need to cleanse your system and unblock those lungs."

When she was done with him, she handed my father a printout listing some syrups and pills she offered for sale.

After my own eye scan, she told me I had an imbalance in my uterus.

Had I ever missed any periods? Had I taken a pregnancy test?

My father, who'd been examining a catalog filled with pricey herbs, suddenly looked up.

"I have no reason to take a pregnancy test," I told her. "My husband and I, well, we're not trying."

My father opened his mouth to say something, but his words dissolved into a long coughing spell, which led her to add a few more recommended items to his list.

"Something's going on with you," she told me, as we left with two hundred dollars' worth of vitamins, coenzymes, liquid oxygen, and natural cough suppressants for my father. "The eyes don't lie."

Dr. Padman's office was a sad and desperate place. Everyone in his waiting room, mostly Caribbean, African, and Eastern European immigrants, seemed to be struggling for breath. Some, like my father, were barely managing on their own, while others dragged mobile oxygen tanks behind them.

My brother Bob, who taught global studies at a nearby high school, was, because of his location and the free afternoons his work schedule allowed, my father's most frequent waiting room companion. After a few visits, however, he too began dreading that gray and dingy room, its stale and stuffy smells, its peeling beige paint and anti-smoking posters, because it was the one place where our father's predicament was most unambiguous, where his future seemed most uncertain. At the same time, it was where Papa appeared most comfortable, where he could cough without being embarrassed, because others were coughing too, some even more vociferously. In the skeletal faces and winded voices around him, he could place himself on some kind of continuum, one where he was still coming out ahead.

A nurse asked my father to step on a scale soon after we arrived. This was the part of the visits he would come to dread most, for it offered proof that he was indeed shrinking. Before he became ill he had carried 170 pounds on his five-eleven frame. During that July 2004 visit he weighed 128 pounds.

When we stepped into his office, Dr. Padman quickly introduced himself. A short, bespectacled South Asian man with only a trace of an accent, he seemed, like my father and me, to have spent part of his life in a section of the world that still echoed in his voice. With the examining table and a full-size scale filling up the tiny room, there was space for only one seat across from his desk, where a computer screen was angled toward a barred window, away from the patient.

I stood behind my father's chair and looked down at both him and the doctor, like a workplace inspector taking everything in while doing her best not to interfere.

"How are you doing, sir?" Dr. Padman asked.

"Not so good," my father answered.

Throughout his illness, my father never told his doctors he was feeling "bad." It was either "Not so good" or "Not so bad," a literal translation of the Creole expression "Pa pi mal."

"And how is the cough, sir?" Dr. Padman continued.

My father replied, "The same."

I wondered whether Dr. Padman's calling my father "sir" was an affectation, a point of effort in his bedside, or deskside, manner or something he did naturally. Maybe he was one of those people who called everyone "sir," especially those who were least likely to be addressed that way. Or maybe it was simply a way of not having to remember names.

Dr. Padman quickly scanned the computer screen, then pulled my father's X-rays and CAT scan film out of a mustard yellow envelope. He held them up to the window light, then, glancing at the computer screen, asked my father, "Are you still on the codeine, sir?"

My father had stopped taking the codeine, which an emergency room physician had prescribed for him, because the codeine had caused him to fail the yearly drug test required by the Taxi and Limousine Commission for the renewal of his cabdriver's license. He took advantage of Dr. Padman's question to ask if Dr. Padman would write a letter for his Taxi and Limousine Commission appeal, stating that he was taking the codeine for legitimate medicinal purposes.

Dr. Padman nodded and made a note on a yellow pad. Then he picked up the phone and buzzed his assistant.

Edie was a skinny, perky Filipina who spoke every sentence at the top of her voice, as though it were being broadcast through a bullhorn at a pep rally.

"Good afternoon," she bellowed, startling my father.

"Edie's going to check your breathing, sir," Dr. Padman told my father.

My father looked up at Edie, then back at the doctor with equal helplessness. He slowly pushed himself up by holding the back of the chair.

"We won't be long," Edie said, grabbing hold of one of my father's elbows.

As my father disappeared from view, I slipped into the

chair where he'd been sitting and tried to sneak a look at Dr. Padman's computer, but the tilt of his screen was designed to give maximum view to the doctor and limited view to the patient.

"Edie is going to do a pulmonary function test," he explained. "The test will require your father to blow into a tube so we can find out how much air is in the lungs."

I imagined my father with this tube in his mouth, trying to fill it impossibly with air and failing over and over again. One did not have to be a pulmonologist to see that he couldn't even blow out a small candle. He had no air to spare.

"I'm really worried about my father," I said.

Perhaps thinking I was talking only about the test, he said, "Don't worry. Edie will take good care of him."

"In general," I said. "I'm worried about his condition."

"Your father has a very bad disease," he said. "It's called pulmonary fibrosis. You can look it up on the Internet. You'll see it's not very good."

Suddenly it was as though we were discussing someone both of us barely knew. I almost expected to go home and look up the disease and find my father's name listed under its many definitions and examples. With no better choices of words, deeds, or prayers, I resorted to a cliché, a common line from soap opera sickrooms.

"What's his prognosis?" I asked.

"It depends on a lot of things," he said, "but most people who are resistant to treatment live anywhere from six months to two years."

My father's body was resisting treatment. The codeine

and prednisone he'd been prescribed by the emergency room physician were neither relieving his cough nor slowing down the gradually irreversible stiffening and scarring of his lungs.

"You should tell your loved ones about your father's condition," Dr. Padman said, as though this was the kind of information one could keep to oneself.

Was this the standard way to tell a family member (without the patient's permission) that the patient was dying? Perhaps he didn't want to add to my father's stress by telling him directly that his disease was incurable. Later, however, he would plainly write it in his letter for my father's appeal to the Taxi and Limousine Commission: "My patient André Miracin Danticat suffers from an incurable condition for which he is required to take codeine."

My father never discussed the letter either before or after he xeroxed it and sent the original to the Taxi and Limousine Commission, which denied his appeal.

What causes an illness like this? I wondered as Dr. Padman and I waited for my father to return from his pulmonary function test. Could it be the persistent car fumes from the twenty-five-plus years my father had worked as a cabdriver? Carcinogens from the twenty-plus years he smoked as a young man, even though he hadn't smoked in more than twenty-five years?

"What about a lung transplant?" I asked Dr. Padman. "Could my father have a lung transplant?"

"He's sixty-nine years old," he said, as though this too was news to me. "I'm afraid he's past the age where he'd be put on the list. Besides, the transplant is no guarantee. There's a very high probability of rejection."

"Can he have surgery to cut out the bad part of the lung and leave the rest?" I asked.

"Both lungs in their entirety are scarred."

I was beginning to feel that whatever I told him would be countered by some unworkable obstruction.

I heard my father's shoes dragging across the floor, heading back toward us. I had come to recognize the sound of his loafers since he'd stopped lifting his feet while walking, to alleviate the pressure of literally having to carry his own weight.

Edie was standing behind him when he appeared in the doorway. Her shoulders drooping, she momentarily seemed as breathless as my father, who had been unable to get through the test. Each time she asked him to breathe into the tube, she reported, he would nearly collapse from coughing.

In the past two months or so, when my father stood for too long, his body would shake as though he might suddenly fall over. His body was shaking now. I got up and helped him into the chair across from the doctor, whom I expected to begin talking again, explaining my father's condition to him. Surely he had only been practicing on me and was going to also tell my father, how "bad" the disease was, how many months he might have left to live.

He didn't. Instead he prescribed more prednisone and codeine. My father didn't say anything. He pushed his head back against the wall, closed his eyes and tried to take deep breaths, which came out as gasps.

.   .   .

Going down in the hospital elevator, still not fully under-standing all that had taken place, I kept my eyes on the flash-ing numbers and avoided looking at my father, who even before he was sick had always been uneasy in unfamiliar sur-roundings. Now he seemed even more apprehensive, lost in the isolated world of the unwell.

In the car I broached again the very first question Dr. Pad-man had posed to him.

"How do you feel, Papa?" I asked in Creole. "Ki jan w santi w?"

Nou la, he said. Not bad. Okay, even. Not by usual stan-dards, but what he'd come to consider okay. Not coughing too much. Not breathing too hard. Driving was fine because he was not exerting too much energy, but walking was diffi-cult. Walking was hell.

"I'm going to drop you off. I'll be home a little bit later," he said as we approached his and my mother's house, a four-bedroom, two-story brick single-family they'd purchased eighteen years ago, after living in a series of small apartments all over Brooklyn.

"Come home and rest," I said.

He had a meeting at the car service business he ran with my uncle Franck, the younger of his two brothers and the only one of his four surviving siblings living in the United States.

My stomach was cramping again, so hard and so fre-quently that I wondered if perhaps the herbalist might be right after all. Was something going on with me? I asked my father to drop me off at a nearby pharmacy, where I picked up a pregnancy test.

. . .

My mother wasn't home when I got there, so I locked myself in my parents' tiny guest bathroom and let a stream of urine run over one of the two plastic sticks in the package. The frosted glass on the bathroom window kept out the afternoon light, and the small space, crowded with my mother's vases of dried roses and potpourri bowls, seemed dark, even with the light on. I squinted to examine the results. One pink line popped up, then two. I examined the box again to make sure I was interpreting correctly. One line meant not pregnant, two meant pregnant, a symbolism that of course made sense. Before the results, one believed oneself to be one; then suddenly one was two.

I leaned against the sink, grabbing hold of the faucet so I could remain on my feet. *My father was dying and I was pregnant.* Both struck me as impossibly unreal.

Cradling the now wet plastic wand, I slipped to the floor and sobbed. I was afraid of losing my father and also struck with a different kind of fear: baby panic. Everything was suddenly mixed up in my head and leading me to the darkest places. Would I carry to full term? Would there be complications? Would I die? Would the baby die? Would the baby and I both die? Would my father die before we died? Or would we all die at the same time?

On the other hand, bringing a child into the world seemed to be about anything *but* death. It was a huge leap of faith in the future, an acknowledgment that one would somehow continue to exist.

I had to speak to my husband. I blindly searched my purse for my cell phone and dialed his number.

"Guess what?" I blurted out. "We're pregnant."

Under different circumstances, I might have rushed back home, greeting him at the airport with an armful of roses addressed to "Daddy." Or I might have teased him on the phone, forced him to pry the news out of me. But there was no other way to do it on this particular day. Still, I held back from telling him about my father. Perhaps I didn't want to hear myself say it. Or maybe I didn't want to dampen his excitement, to have these two pieces of news abruptly collide for him as they had for me.

"A baby? How wonderful is that?" My husband was cheering loudly. I could imagine his calm, reassuring smile, broader with delight.

"I can't believe it," he shouted, after it had sunk in a bit longer. "We're going to be parents!"

Aside from my husband, I decided, I would tell no one about the baby for a few days, not even my parents. That weekend, my brother Kelly, a musician and computer programmer, who out of all of us most resembled my father, was coming for a visit from his home in Lancaster, Massachusetts. We all needed to concentrate on a family strategy to deal with my father's diagnosis and we were not going to come up with one if everyone was distracted by the baby. Besides, I couldn't fully keep both realities in mind at the same time, couldn't find the words to express both events. I closed my eyes and held my breath, forcing myself to recite it as a mantra. *My father is dying and I'm pregnant.*

I stepped out of the bathroom and called my youngest brother, Karl, at the brokerage house where he works. I told him what Dr. Padman had said, and immediately a debate emerged: Should the doctor have told me about our father's prognosis and not have told our father? It was inconsiderate at best, Karl thought, and maybe even unethical.

"It seems odd." He sounded infuriated: at me, at the doctor, at the diagnosis, at the disease. "The doctor has no right to share information with you that he's withholding from Dad."

Maybe I shouldn't have called him at work, I thought. I should have waited until he got home. There was always so much happening in his office. People were always peeking in; his phone was always ringing. He was probably under pressure. I had sprung this on him out of nowhere, told him too quickly, and he'd had no choice but to respond from the gut, unfiltered.

Of the four of us, my brothers Karl and Bob, who lived only a few blocks away from my parents' house in East Flatbush, saw my father most often. They, more than anyone, except maybe my mother, were going to have to watch him die.

"Are you going to tell Dad what the doctor said?" Karl asked, his voice firm, terse.

"No," I said, equally unyielding.

I hadn't decided until that moment that I wouldn't have that conversation with my father. Maybe Karl or my other brothers could, or even my mother would, but I knew I wouldn't be able to do it. I now found myself rallying on Dr. Padman's side. What would be the use of telling Dad? He would probably become disheartened, heartbroken, depressed. On the other hand, he was a religious man. Maybe he would refute his prognosis outright, call it a lie, and not believe it at all. Still, I didn't think I'd be able to tell him. Maybe it was cowardly, but I couldn't.

"We should tell Dad what the doctor said," Karl insisted. "He should have been told. He has a right to know. Wouldn't you want to know?"

Of course I'd want to know. I agreed with him in principle. But suddenly I wondered: if my father ever found out some other way, would he interpret both the doctor's and my not telling him as a sign that things were even more dismal than they actually were?

That afternoon, before my father came home, as my mother prepared his supper I told her a milder version of what Dr. Padman had told me.

"The doctor doesn't think he's doing well," I said as she cut up a small squash and slipped the pieces into a pot of boiling water to make a stew. "The doctor says he might not recover."

I kept needlessly repeating the word "doctor" as if to stress that I was the messenger and not the source.

Securing the lid on the pot, my mother turned off the burners on the stove, poured herself a glass of water from the leaky faucet over the sink and sat down across from me at the bare kitchen table.

"I knew it was something bad," she said, massaging the sides of her round face with her fingers. Her voice was soft, slow, almost a whisper. "He just seems to be melting away."

What she cooked that night was a much simpler version of

what she'd originally intended, a thin pumpkin soup rather than a full stew. The soup remained untouched, however. None of us felt like eating.

A few days later, my father's church's deacon association hosted its yearly anniversary brunch at an all-you-can-eat Chinese buffet restaurant on Ralph Avenue in Canarsie, Brooklyn. My father's ivory suit was so big on him that, as he'd put it on that morning, he'd added two more holes to his belt, which, overstretched, looked like scarred skin.

Dragging his gaunt frame between the tables to greet dozens of longtime friends, he seemed buoyant and jovial, but after each handshake and brief chat he had to lay his hand on someone's shoulder to rest.

When he was done with his round of greetings, he filled a plate with fried chicken wings he never touched. As he coughed, some of the church members came over and held his hand. Others urged him to go home. They might have meant well, but he felt rejected. As if they didn't want him near their food.

That same afternoon, my brother Kelly arrived from Massachusetts, so my father decided to hold a family meeting. That meeting, like all my father's rare previous summits, was a rather formal affair. As we all sat around my parents' long oak dining room table, framed by my mother's ornately carved, antique-looking but brand-new china and enlarged photographs of our school graduations, weddings and Christmases, my father went directly to the matter at hand.

"The reason for this gathering," he announced, "is to discuss what is going to happen to your mother after I'm gone."

My father was sitting in his usual seat at the head of the table. My mother was on the other end facing him. I was sitting on his left, her right, with Karl, who, at six foot one, towered over all of us. Kelly and Bob, the middle children, as I liked to call them, were sitting across from us. We were all stunned into silence by my father's pronouncement, both those among us who thought we should recount to him what the doctor had said (brothers Karl and Kelly) and the rest of us who did not. But maybe the doctor was the wisest of any of us. Of course the patient always knows. My father must have suspected even before the doctor had. After all, he inhabited the body that was failing.

"I'm not getting better." My father covered his face with his hands, then slowly pulled them apart as though he were opening a book. "And when a person's sick, either you're getting better or you're dying."

He said this so casually and with so little sorrow that my sadness was momentarily lifted.

"What would you like to happen after I'm gone?" he asked, looking directly at my mother. "Do you want to stay in the house, or sell it and buy an apartment?"

"I'm not going anywhere," my mother said defiantly.

A line of sweat was growing over her lips as she spoke. I appreciated her unwillingness to embark for such an unknown world, to look toward another life, beyond her husband's.

"The house might be too big for you to live in by yourself," my father continued, matter-of-factly. "Someone would have to move in with you."

I kept my eyes on the sheer plastic sheath that covered my mother's hibiscus-embroidered tablecloth. Was my father trying to prepare us? Put us at ease? Show us that we shouldn't worry about him, or was he trying to tell us that he was ready for whatever lay ahead?

"Pop." Bob rubbed his eyes with his balled fists, then raised his hands to catch my father's attention. While I'd been staring at the tablecloth, he'd been crying.

"Pop, can I ask you a question?" The tears were flowing down Bob's face. He was easily the huskiest and the most overtly emotional of my three brothers, Karl being the most levelheaded and Kelly the most reserved.

"What is your question?" my father asked, his own eyes growing moist, though he was doing his best to hold back his tears.

"Have you enjoyed your life?" Bob asked, pausing after each word as if to take in its weight and meaning.

I lowered my head again, absorbing the stillness that also followed this question, the kind of hush that suddenly forces you to pay attention to so many unrelated things around you: the shell of the dead fly trapped in the window screen, the handprints on the plastic over the tablecloth, the ticking of a giant clock in the next room, the pressing desire for anything, including an explosion, to burst forth and disrupt the calm.

"I don't know what to say about that." My father drew in his breath, something that required a great deal of effort and thus resulted in a grimace-like contortion of his face. "I don't—I can't—remember every moment. But what I can say is this. I haven't enjoyed myself in the sense of party and glory. I haven't seen a lot of places and haven't done that many things, but I've had a good life."

My father went on to list what he considered his greatest accomplishments: Kelly, Karl, Bob and me, as well as his three grandchildren, Karl's five-year-old son Ezekiel and two-year-old daughter Zora and Bob's five-year-old daughter Nadira.

"You, my children, have not shamed me," he continued. "I'm proud of that. It could have been so different. Edwidge and Bob, your mother and I left you behind for eight years in Haiti. Kelly and Karl, you grew up here, in a country your mother and I didn't know very well when we had you. You all could have turned bad, but you didn't. I thank God for that. I thank God for all of you. I thank God for your mother." Then turning his eyes back to Bob, he added, "Yes, you can say I have enjoyed my life."

Listening to my father, I remembered a time when I used to dream of smuggling him words. I was eight years old and Bob and I were living in Haiti with his oldest brother, my uncle Joseph, and his wife. And since they didn't have a telephone at home—few Haitian families did then—and access to the call centers was costly, we had no choice but to write letters. Every other month, my father would mail a half-page, three-paragraph missive addressed to my uncle. Scribbled in his minuscule scrawl, sometimes on plain white paper, other times on lined, hole-punched notebook pages still showing bits of fringe from the spiral binding, my father's letters were composed in stilted French, with the first paragraph offering news of his and my mother's health, the second detailing how to spend the money they had wired for food, lodging, and school expenses for Bob and myself, the third section concluding abruptly after reassuring us that we'd be hearing from him again before long.

Later I would discover in a first-year college composition class that his letters had been written in a diamond sequence, the Aristotelian *Poetics* of correspondence, requiring an opening greeting, a middle detail or request, and a brief farewell at the end. The letter-writing process had been such an agonizing chore for my father, one that he'd hurried through while assembling our survival money, that this specific epistolary formula, which he followed unconsciously, had offered him a comforting way of disciplining his emotions.

"I was no writer," he later told me. "What I wanted to tell you and your brother was too big for any piece of paper and a small envelope."

Whatever restraint my father showed in his letters was easily compensated for by Uncle Joseph's reactions to them. First there was the public reading in my uncle's sparsely furnished pink living room, in front of Tante Denise, Bob and me. This was done so there would be no misunderstanding as to how the money my parents sent for me and my brother would be spent. Usually my uncle would read the letters out loud, pausing now and then to ask my help with my father's penmanship, a kindness, I thought, a way to include me a step further. It soon became obvious, however, that my father's handwriting was as clear to me as my own, so I eventually acquired the job of deciphering his letters.

Along with this task came a few minutes of preparation for the reading and thus a few intimate moments with my father's letters, not only the words and phrases, which did not vary greatly from month to month, but the vowels and syllables, their tilts and slants, which did. Because he wrote so little, I would try to guess his thoughts and moods from the dotting of his *i*'s and the crossing of his *t*'s, from whether there were actual periods at the ends of his sentences or just faint dots where the tip of his pen had simply landed. Did commas split his streamlined phrases, or were they staccato, like someone speaking too rapidly, out of breath?

For the family readings, I recited my father's letters in a monotone, honoring what I interpreted as a secret between us, that the impersonal style of his letters was due as much to his lack of faith in words and their ability to accurately reproduce his emotions as to his caution with Bob's and my feelings, avoiding too-happy news that might add to the anguish of separation, too-sad news that might worry us, and any hint of judgment or disapproval for my aunt and uncle, which they could have interpreted as suggestions that they were mistreating us. The dispassionate letters were his way of avoiding a minefield, one he could have set off from a distance without being able to comfort the victims.

Given all this anxiety, I'm amazed my father wrote at all. The regularity, the consistency of his correspondence now feels like an act of valor. In contrast, my replies, though less routine—Uncle Joseph did most of the writing—were both painstakingly upbeat and suppliant. In my letters, I bragged about my good grades and requested, as a reward for them, an American doll at Christmas, a typewriter or sewing machine for my birthday, a pair of "real" gold earrings for Easter. But the things I truly wanted I was afraid to ask for, like when

I would finally see him and my mother again. However, since my uncle read and corrected all my letters for faulty grammar and spelling, I wrote for his eyes more than my father's, hoping that even after the vigorous editing, my father would still decode the longing in my childish cursive slopes and arches, which were so much like his own.

The words that both my father and I wanted to exchange we never did. These letters were not approved, in his case by him, in my case by my uncle. No matter what the reason, we have always been equally paralyzed by the fear of breaking each other's heart. This is why I could never ask the question Bob did. I also could never tell my father that I'd learned from the doctor that he was dying. Even when they mattered less, there were things he and I were too afraid to say.

A few days after the family meeting, my father called my uncle Joseph in Haiti, to see how he was doing. It was Thursday, July 15, 2004, the fifty-first birthday of Jean-Bertrand Aristide, Haiti's twice-elected and twice-deposed president. Having been removed from power in February 2004 through a joint political action by France, Canada and the United States, Aristide was now spending his birthday in exile in South Africa. However, the residents of Bel Air, the neighborhood where I grew up and where my uncle Joseph still lived, had not forgotten him. Joining other Aristide supporters, they'd marched, nearly three thousand of them, through the Haitian capital to call for his return. The march had been mostly peaceful, except that, according to the television news reports that my father and I had watched together that evening, two policemen had been shot. My father called my uncle, just as he always did whenever something like this was happening in Haiti. He was sitting up in bed, his head propped on two firm pillows, his face angled toward the bedroom window, which allowed him a slanted view of a neighborhood street lamp.

"Are you sure he's sleeping?" my father asked whoever had answered the phone at my uncle's house in Bel Air.

My father cupped the phone with one hand, pushed his face toward me and whispered, "Maxo."

I gathered he was talking to Uncle Joseph's son, Maxo, who had left Haiti in the early 1970s to attend college in New York, then had returned in 1995. Though I had spent most of my childhood with Maxo's son Nick, I did not know Maxo as well.

"Don't you think it's time your father moved out of Bel Air?" my father asked Maxo.

As he hung up, he seemed disappointed that he hadn't been able to speak to Uncle Joseph. Over the years, this had been a touchy subject between my father and uncle: my father wanting my uncle to move to another part, any other part, of Haiti and my uncle refusing to even consider it. I now imagined my father longing to tell his brother to leave Bel Air, but this time not for the reasons he usually offered—the constant demonstrations, the police raids and gang wars that caused him to constantly worry—but because my father was dying and he wanted his oldest brother to be safe.

I write these things now, some as I witnessed them and today remember them, others from official documents, as well as the borrowed recollections of family members. But the gist of them was told to me over the years, in part by my uncle Joseph, in part by my father. Some were told offhand, quickly. Others, in greater detail. What I learned from my father and uncle, I learned out of sequence and in fragments. This is an attempt at cohesiveness, and at re-creating a few wondrous and terrible months when their lives and mine intersected in startling ways, forcing me to look forward and back at the same time. I am writing this only because they can't.

Brother, I'm Dying

S omething broke the first time my uncle Joseph met his wife, in May 1946. It was barely dawn, a gray morning over the blue-green hills of Beauséjour. The sun was slowly rising, burning through the fog that merged with the clouds over the highest mountains. My uncle, oval-faced, with a widow's-peaked hairline, mustached and pudgy, as he would remain for most of his life, was making his way down the winding trail that joined the village where he and his parents and five younger brothers and sisters lived, with the market town in the valley below. He had started from his parents' farm with a mule loaded with carrots and plantains and newly harvested pigeon peas that he planned to sell at the market. Running late, he tapped the mule's bottom now and then, encouraging it to hasten its steps. It wasn't doing much good. The mule was tired and seemed to want to stop and sniff each patch of dew-laden grass and muddy rock it encountered along the way.

Uncle Joseph was growing exasperated when he spotted a

young woman on the same path. With her high cheekbones and pouty lips she looked like a calendar girl or carnival queen. She was wearing a thin cotton dress, which seemed glued to her body by the water still lingering from the early-morning bath she'd just taken in a nearby stream. On top of her head was a brown calabash, sealed with a piece of dried corn husk. The calabash was resting on a piece of cloth, wrung into a circle to serve as a base. Ignoring the mule, he stopped to watch her. She was one of the prettiest women he'd come across in his twenty-three years. How could he not have spotted her during all his trips to and from the market?

Unsupervised, the mule wandered into a nearby garden and spilled some of my uncle's merchandise. The young lady was the one who first noticed the mule stomping through a row of young cocoa plants. Rushing forward, she motioned in its direction. As her body swayed back and forth, her arms waving wildly, she dropped her water-filled calabash and it broke.

My uncle offered to pay for the calabash. She insisted it was not necessary, but he talked her into taking a few pennies, a lot more than the calabash was worth.

"So began a conversation between Denise and me," my uncle later told me. "Every time I went by afterwards on my way to the market, I had to see her. We talked and talked for a few months and then we took action."

The action was to notify their families at the beginning of 1947 that they were moving to the capital together. The oldest of his sisters, my aunt Ino, was already living in Bel Air, a hilltop neighborhood overlooking Port-au-Prince harbor, and they decided to settle there.

Though they did not marry, they bought a plot of land together and built a three-room cement house, topped by a corrugated-metal roof. The house had a large front gallery that extended into the alley that curved toward the main road, Rue Tirremasse. The entire house was painted salmon pink, both inside and out, except for the floors, which were covered with terra-cotta clay tiles.

The hill in Bel Air on which the house was built had been the site of a famous battle between mulatto abolitionists and French colonists who'd controlled most of the island since 1697 and had imported black Africans to labor on coffee and sugar plantations as slaves. A century later, slaves and mulattoes joined together to drive the French out, and on January 1, 1804, formed the Republic of Haiti.

More than a century later, as World War I dawned and the French, British and Germans, who controlled Haiti's international shipping, rallied their gunboats to protect their interests, President Woodrow Wilson, whose interests included, among others, the United Fruit Company and 40 percent of the stock of the Haitian national bank, ordered an invasion. When the U.S. Marines landed in Haiti in July 1915 for what would become a nineteen-year occupation, Haitian guerrilla fighters, called Cacos, organized attacks against the U.S. forces from Bel Air. Bel Air also boasted one of Haiti's oldest and most beautiful cathedrals, as well as one of the island's best public schools for boys, the Lycée Pétion, which was named after Alexandre Pétion, one of the leaders in the battle for independence from the French and a mentor to Venezuela's Simón Bolívar.

When he first moved to Bel Air, my uncle got a job

working as a salesman for a Syrian émigré in a fabric shop in downtown Port-au-Prince. There he befriended a fellow salesman, a Cuban émigré named Guillermo Hernandez, who quickly became his best friend. A few months later, my father, then twelve years old, left Beauséjour and moved to the capital to attend school there. My aunts Zi and Tina and Uncle Franck later joined them, along with my grandparents, Granpè Nozial and Granmè Lorvana, who went to live with Tante Ino, the eldest daughter. Encouraged by my uncle, nearly everyone they knew was now living in Bel Air. He and Tante Denise kept adding to the house until it had six bedrooms, still pink. So when their son, Maxo, was born in 1948 there was room for him. And in 1952 there was also room when the Haitian wife of Guillermo Hernandez, his Cuban friend, died, leaving Guillermo with a six-month-old baby to raise alone. It was Guillermo who asked my uncle and Tante Denise to take in his daughter, Marie Micheline, so he could travel back home to Cuba for a visit, a trip from which he never returned.

Uncle Joseph's hero in the 1950s was a politician named Daniel Fignolé. Uncle Joseph liked to recount how as a young legislator, Fignolé went to the public hospital in Port-au-Prince, and finding poor patients lying on the floor while the rich patients recovered in beds, he forced the rich off the beds and gave them to the poor. Soon after my uncle moved to Bel Air, Fignolé started the Laborers and Peasants Party (Mouvement Ouvriers-Paysans), which my uncle joined. For years, he and Tante Denise opened their house to Fignolé sympathizers for regular meetings, which were lively affairs

with plenty of homemade liquor—kleren—and food prepared by Tante Denise, who everyone in their circle agreed
was one of the best cooks in Bel Air. When it came time to
address the fifty or so people who'd gathered in his pink living room, kept sparsely furnished to fit in the largest possible
number of Fignolists, who often brought their own chairs
with them, he would model Fignolé's forceful and direct Creole diction and speak in a clear, powerful bass, allowing only
a few well-chosen pauses.

"We have struggled since we became an independent
nation in 1804," my uncle recalled saying. "Certain people
think that in order for the country to progress, only the rich
minority need succeed. This country cannot move forward
without the majority. Without us."

Hardly earth-shattering, but he considered himself more
of a disciple than a chief. All he had to do was echo one of
Fignolé's favorite phrases to get applause.

In his speeches to the group, my uncle sometimes evoked
his father, Granpè Nozial, who'd joined the guerrilla resistance against the U.S. invasion and who was often away
from home fighting a battle he did his best to keep from
reaching his young children. Granpè Nozial would leave my
uncle, the oldest, though still a child himself, the task of
looking after his mother and siblings for weeks and months
at a time. Each time his father left for a campaign, my uncle
worried that, like the thousands of Haitian guerrilla fighters
who were killed by the Americans and whose corpses were
dumped in roads and public parks to discourage others, his
father might never come back.

"The men of my father's generation fought with all their

might," my uncle would declare in a carefully modulated voice as he addressed the Fignolists who'd crowded into his living room, including his father, Granpè Nozial, who, now widowed and looking older than his sixty-five years, sat stoop-shouldered, his once sinewy body beaten and worn, his head bouncing back and forth as he dozed off in the front row.

"But mostly," my uncle continued, "these men used their hands and old-fashioned weapons. They used old Krags, slingshots, machetes and spears. They used whatever weapons they could muster up or create. Now we want to fight for progress. We want to fight with our minds. This is where real power lies."

At that time, the president of Haiti was Paul Magloire, an army general who'd unseated two of his predecessors. Nicknamed Kanson Fé, or Iron Pants, because of a speech he had given in which he'd declared that he must put on "iron pants" to deal with troublemakers, he had graced the February 22, 1954, cover of *Time* magazine dressed in full golden military regalia over a caption that read: "HAITI'S PRESIDENT PAUL MAGLOIRE. His Black Magic: roads, dams, schools."

In 1956 Magloire stepped down after a national strike over, among other things, increased dissatisfaction with his extravagant spending. In addition to roads, dams, and schools, it turned out, he spent lots of money on lavish parties, state visits and costly reenactments of famous Haitian battles, mostly to amuse himself and a small circle of like-minded friends. Fignolé was one of many in a slippery line of succession who would eventually replace him. On May 25, 1957, as Fignolé was sworn into office, my uncle and father were part of the massive crowd that dashed to the national palace to dance in celebration. However, after only nineteen days, Fignolé was deposed by the army and forced into exile. François "Papa Doc" Duvalier then assumed the presidency. Tante Denise woke up the next morning to find Uncle Joseph sobbing in their bed. (My father, then twenty-two years old, has no recollection of his own reaction to all this, only of my uncle's, which was "sad".)

Before Fignolé's fall, my uncle had briefly contemplated running for political office, either as a deputy from Bel Air or as mayor of Port-au-Prince. After Fignolé's ouster, he realized how precarious political power could be and abandoned all notions of being part of it.

Feeling an ideological void, he joined a Baptist congregation that one of his friends belonged to, using the time he would have spent at demonstrations and meetings to go to church. The Baptists offered the promise of a peaceful and stable life. They forbade so many things, including smoking and drinking, that there were few ways for a young man to get in trouble. The Baptists also forbade common-law marriage, so after more than a decade together, when their son Maxo was ten years old, he and Tante Denise finally married in a church ceremony, after which he became a deacon in the church. He then enrolled in a training course for future pastors and while taking the course befriended a group of American missionaries who regularly came to Haiti. He was eager to open his own church and a school. He was still wary of Americans from his memories of the U.S. occupation, but the missionaries were looking to fund a project in his area and he didn't have enough to do it on his own, so he proposed his idea to them and they gave him some money to help with the building, blackboards, and benches and pledged a monthly contribution for a free lunch program for the students.

My uncle bought another plot of land in Bel Air and spent his evenings designing and then building his church. As the building came up from the ground, he would visit the site daily, both before and after his work at the textile shop. He'd stack bricks and mix cement, hammer wood with the workers. He wanted to feel like he was investing more than his heart and mind, that he was investing his hands and feet, his labor too. Because he believed that the church had redeemed him, saved him from a series of potentially hazardous choices, he named it L'Eglise Chrétienne de la Redemption, the Christian Church of Redemption. The shotgun-style, gable-roofed building, which doubled as a classroom and cafeteria during the week, he hoped, would redeem others as well.

As a child living in his house from the time I was four until I was twelve years old, I remember my uncle's voice being crisp and distinct: deep and resolute, breathy and jingly when he was angry, steely and muted when he was sad. When he began preaching sermons, my father recalled, sermons which required that he project a wide range of emotions in one hour or less, my uncle had the same effect on the hundred or so people who attended his church as he'd had on those who crowded into his living room to listen to him talk about Fignolé. Many of them were indeed the same people and were surprised now in the church how much passion he could stir in them.

"His preaching style was very straightforward," remembered my father. "He talked a lot about love. God's love, the love we should have for one another. He knew all the verses for love. Sometimes I'd close my eyes and think, would I want to hear him if he wasn't my brother and I'd have to say yes. Yes, he would have made a very good politician, but my brother was a better preacher."

But one day in November 1977, while preaching a lengthy sermon to commemorate the church's anniversary, my uncle's voice began to quiver, then squeak. He shrieked like an adolescent boy at one moment, then could only moan the next. His throat and gums throbbed and hurt. The next day, he went to the local dentist, who decided he needed to remove all of my uncle's teeth and replace them with dentures.

His voice did not improve even after all his teeth were gone, so he went to see several other doctors. The doctors couldn't find anything wrong, so he went to herbalists, just as his parents and grandparents had before him. He was after all a child of the countryside—nou se moun mòn—and had been treated by roots and leaves most of his life. But the herbalists too were stumped. Meanwhile his voice grew fainter and his throat continued to ache.

One afternoon, in the spring of 1978, he was listening to the radio when he heard about a hospital in the south of Haiti that was associated with a radio station, Radio Lumière. Some American doctors were coming to the hospital and everyone who wanted to was welcome to come for a consultation. My uncle headed out to meet them.

After a day of slow, difficult travel on pitted, rocky roads, the camion he was on broke down in the early evening. Near the town of Gros Marin, he walked into a small two-room house by the side of a road and asked a peasant woman if he could spend the night on her beaten-earth floor. Her quick yes, so typical of the men and women of the Haitian country-side, reminded him of his own childhood. Lying in her front room on a palm frond mat and one of her best sheets, he thought back to a childhood of working in the fields and the palm-covered classrooms with neither walls nor doors where he learned his lessons sitting on the floor. He thought of a thin yet strapping father whose arms were so taut from a life of farming and fighting that he could render you uncon-scious with one slap while not even looking in your direc-tion. He thought of the khakied American marines who he was told ambushed guerrilla resisters like his father in the middle of the night while wearing blackface. The Americans had reinstated forced labor to build bridges and roads and had snatched able-bodied men like his father and boys like himself from their homes. They were lucky to have been spared. So determined was he that he would not be taken that whenever Granpè Nozial was away from home, he'd sleep with a well-sharpened machete under his pillow.

The next morning my uncle was startled out of his sleep by the sound of a sisal broom sweeping the woman's cactus-fenced yard. That gentle sound and the fragrant smell of brewed coffee helped remove his dread, filled him with hope. The woman handed him an enameled basin filled with cold water to wash his face and a handful of mint to brush the dentures she mistook for his own teeth. She then gave him a square of dimpled bread, which looked as though it was made from dough that had been poked with a dozen ice picks. The bread was carefully wrapped in a piece of muslin and lay on a plate that covered a metal cup filled with dark, sweet coffee. His hunger stirred, he gobbled the bread and washed it down with the coffee. He thanked the woman for her kindness and hospitality and with the air still cool from the night and the sun still very low in the sky, he continued on his way.

He had a long wait in the hospital yard. Hundreds of people were milling about, crouched in shaded corners of the concrete building, squatting under the giant almond trees, waiting. He was with men and women who were suffering from tuberculosis, malaria, typhoid fever and other not so easily recognizable afflictions. It had taken him a good part of the morning to walk from the woman's house in Gros Marin to the hospital in Bonne Fin. He waited in the hot sun with the others until midafternoon, sweaty, hungry and thirsty now, hoping he wouldn't be turned back.

At last, he was looked over by a nurse and placed among the least urgent cases. When it was his turn to see a doctor, one of the visiting physicians, a tall white man, pressed his tongue down with a thin wooden stick and told him he saw a mass sitting on top of his larynx. The mass might be a tumor, the doctor explained through a translator, and if not removed could eventually block his airways and suffocate him. He wanted to do a biopsy right away, the doctor said.

"Can you take it out?" my uncle asked.

"We will only do the biopsy now," explained the translator. "We're taking a piece, not the whole thing, but when the entire mass is removed, you might lose your voice."

Stunned, my uncle asked again, just to be sure, "Will I lose my voice today?"

"We'll only do the biopsy today," the doctor repeated.

Before my uncle could ask what a biopsy was, the translator, a Haitian doctor, added, "You have to let them cut a piece of the mass in your throat to examine it for cancer. It might be your only chance."

During the biopsy, for which my uncle was given no more anesthesia than he might have gotten at the dentist's office while having a tooth removed, he opened his mouth so wide that his face and neck throbbed. Lying there as the doctor clipped a piece of flesh from the back of his throat, he wished he could go back home and have one final conversation with his wife. He also wanted to preach one last sermon to his congregation, speak on the phone with his son and to my father in New York.

That evening, after the biopsy, my uncle lay in a hospital bed, unable to speak. Would his voice ever come back? He wrote that question on little pieces of paper the nurses gave him. They told him once more that this time it would, but probably not when he had the actual operation.

The next morning, the doctor explained through another translator that the tumor was cancerous. He needed a radical laryngectomy. His voice box would eventually have to be removed. Yes, he would most certainly lose his voice.

After the doctors left his bedside, my uncle became aware that someone in the hospital bed next to his had a small transistor radio, which was tuned to the same station where he'd first heard about the American doctors. The station had a charter studio on the hospital premises and the sound was coming through loud and clear. Over the airwaves, he heard among the lists of announcements about missing people and lost objects a voice saying, "Reverend Joseph Nosius, please come home. Your family is worried about you."

My uncle was staring at the ceiling and wondering whether the doctors with their "biopsy" had done him more harm than good when he heard the announcer's voice. It reminded him how important voices were. If you had one, you could use it to reach out to your loved ones, no matter how far away. Technological advances could help—the telephone, the radio, microphones, megaphones, amplifiers. But if you had no voice at all, he thought, you were simply left out of the constant hum of the world, the echo of conversations, the shouts and whispers of everyday life.

As he lay there, listening to the other patients talk to the doctors and nurses, to their family members and to each other, it occurred to him that after the operation, he would never again be able to preach a sermon or scream for help or laugh out loud at a funny joke. He also knew he had to get word to Tante Denise that he was alive.

Slowly he sat up and wrote a brief message on a piece of paper by his bedside and gave it to one of the nurses to take to the station studio for him. The message simply asked if they could let his wife know that he was all right at the hospital and would be home soon.

When the doctors came back to see him that afternoon, they told him they couldn't operate and remove the tumor. It was too large and they didn't have the right equipment for the procedure. They asked if he had any family or friends abroad. He said that both his son and his brother, my father, were living in New York. The doctor gave him a copy of his medical file and wrote a letter for him to take to the American consulate requesting a visa to travel for the surgery.

When my uncle returned home to Bel Air and, in a hoarser voice than he'd left with, tried to explain his diagnosis to his wife, his congregation, and even on the telephone to my father and Maxo, with whom he was planning to stay in New York, no one quite understood it. None of our relatives knew what a radical laryngectomy was. We didn't even know anyone who'd had cancer. As for permanently losing one's voice, the possibility seemed so remote that it almost appeared to be a curse that, as some of the members of my uncle's congregation declared, only American doctors could cross an ocean to put on you. People were either born mute or not. They did not become mute, except temporarily if they were struck with a bad case of shock. Usually those cases could be easily cured with herbal remedies. Why not my uncle's?

To put everyone at ease, my uncle said that maybe the doctors in New York would know more. Maybe he would discover other options, other solutions. Nevertheless, he gathered all his papers—land titles, everyone's birth certificates—made out a will, and turned everything over to the daughter of his friend, then twenty-six-year-old Marie Micheline, whom he'd adopted and made his own. He wanted desperately to take Tante Denise to New York with him, but there were two problems. First, she was deathly afraid of flying. Then, because the likelihood of his returning to Haiti increased with his having a wife there to return to, her visa request was denied by the American consulate. Uncle Joseph and Tante Denise hadn't spent much time apart since he'd broken her calabash thirty-two years before. However, time was of the essence, so he had no choice but to travel without her, even though he feared that he might die and never see her again.

.

In New York, Uncle Joseph had been at his son Maxo's apartment for barely twenty-four hours when he woke up in the middle of the night with a sharp, throbbing pain in his neck.

Maxo was out with a friend. Uncle Joseph somehow managed to stumble out of bed and over to the only phone in the apartment, which was in the kitchen. He dialed my father's number. My father was living in East Flatbush, three subway stops, a thirty-minute walk and a fifteen-minute drive from Maxo's place on Ocean Avenue. My uncle heard a crackling as my father's phone was picked up.

"Hello," my father said, his voice creaking anxiously. No good news could ever come at this hour of the night, he told himself.

My uncle pressed his lips as close as he could to the mouthpiece to whisper these three words: "Frè, map mouri." Brother, I'm dying.

"What's wrong?" my father asked.

"Gòj," he replied. Throat.

My father told him to open the front door to the apartment and wait. Then he hung up and called an ambulance. When he called back, Uncle Joseph didn't answer, so my father got dressed, jumped into his car and sped toward the apartment building where my uncle was staying.

The paramedics made it there before he did. When they

arrived, they found Uncle Joseph lying on the floor near the front door, barely conscious, clutching his neck, gasping for breath. They tried to put a breathing tube down his throat, but the tumor was blocking his airway. So while racing toward Kings County Hospital, they performed a tracheotomy, drilling a hole in my uncle's neck to insert a tube there so he could breathe.

My uncle had his radical laryngectomy the next day. When he came out, he was never able to use his own voice again. He was fifty-five years old.

My uncle's operation cost around thirty thousand dollars, which was negotiated down and paid for by his American missionary friends.

As my uncle recovered at Maxo's house, my father advised him to remain in New York for a few months to make sure he was in remission. But he wouldn't listen.

"What about my church?" he scribbled on a piece of paper. "My wife? Besides, this was not a good first visit to New York. Not enjoyable."

So as soon as the doctors cleared him a month later, he packed his bags and returned to Haiti.

"Our lives were now even more solidly on different tracks," my father would later recall. "He believed that his life had been spared for some reason and only in Haiti could he discover why. He could have moved to New York when Maxo and I came and he could have moved after that. But I don't think he ever really wanted to leave Bel Air for any place in or outside of Haiti."

What Did the White Man Say?

I told my parents I was pregnant in my father's car, on the way to the airport. It was more than a week after I learned my father's diagnosis. But whenever I found myself alone with him and my mother, I simply couldn't find the words.

I came close to telling them the night before I had to return to Miami. I was sitting on my father's bed watching television when my mother came in and sat down on the edge of the bed next to me. I opened my mouth and thought the words came out, but they hadn't.

The time limit on the car ride would make it easier, I told myself. If I wanted to tell them in person there would be no other opportunity to do so.

This was not the first time I was sharing important news with my parents in this way. I had rattled off the list of colleges I'd been accepted to in the car one Sunday morning on the way to church. I'd announced my engagement on the way to a cousin's wedding one Saturday afternoon. This manner of sharing important information annoyed my father, who, before his diagnosis, had never mentioned anything monumental in a casual way.

"We have to chat," he'd announce days before actually sharing news.

"There's something we need to discuss," he'd remind me hours later.

"Let me know when you have some time," he'd say until we'd finally sit down for a brief but formal talk.

The best place for me to make my announcement would have been at the family meeting the week before. This is probably what both my parents would have expected, and preferred, rather than my spitting something out and scurrying off. But that night I couldn't look into my father's face and—though I knew it would come very naturally to him and my mother both—ask that they be happy for me.

The trip from my parents' house to the airport normally takes about a half hour at midday. I allowed ten minutes to lapse, while waiting for my father to catch his breath from the effort of walking from the house to his car.

"I can take a cab, Papa," I'd said as I piled in ahead of my mother, who didn't drive, but even if she did, would have probably not been given the wheel by my father.

His body hunched over, my father placed his head close to the dashboard. He was still panting and unable to reply, but shook his head in protest as he fired up the ignition. Before he became sick, I might have said of my father that driving for him was like breathing. The night before, I had calculated that from 1981 to 2004, working an average ten hours every day, including holidays but not Sundays, he'd spent nearly seventy-five thousand hours driving the streets of Brooklyn.

I knew my father had momentarily recovered from the panting when he asked what my mother had cooked for me to take back with me to Miami.

Whenever I visited my parents, my mother would send me back with an overnight bag filled with food. She'd wake up early the morning of my trip to make sure I had several containers filled with fried snapper, sweet potato cake, codfish patties, a large bag of plantain chips and several packages of cassava bread. My mother, opulently full-figured, broad-shouldered, always presented me with this bounty at the very last minute, sometimes as we pulled up to the curb at the airport. Her food and my father's ride were part of a send-off that often left me feeling guilty and scared, guilty for leaving them behind and scared that something awful, a stroke or a heart attack, might befall them in my absence.

"What did your mother give you this time?" my father asked.

Having watched my mother pack the bag of food, he knew. But he asked anyway, as he always did, in a half-joking manner, in part to tease my mother about her longing, which she'd perhaps carried since I was a child, to feed me from afar.

I told them between the winding, narrow lanes of the Jackie Robinson Parkway. My father's old red Lincoln was too wide for one lane, especially at the curves, so he took up both lanes, angering the drivers who couldn't pass him. Gripping the wheel tightly, he seemed to block the other drivers out as they honked loudly and poked their heads out of windows to curse him. As my father zigzagged around the curves with an angry army of drivers behind him, I told them. I think now that this showed a great deal of confidence in his driving. I must have trusted completely that nothing could have an impact on it.

"I have some news," I began.

My father was sitting on a square cushion to shield his bony bottom from the painful bumps on the roads, his elbow leaning on the armrest separating him from my mother and me.

My voice cracked. All of a sudden I couldn't help but think of an alternate scenario, making this happy announcement to an unsick father. Perhaps we might have still found ourselves driving on a curvy road on the way to an airport, but my only unease might have been the mild sense of embarrassment one feels having a sex-related conversation, however celebratory, with one's parents.

"I'm pregnant," I mumbled.

"Sa blan an di?" asked my mother. What did the blan say?

This was the way my mother always let my brothers and me know she hadn't heard or understood something we'd said. The equivalent of a gringo, a blan was not just a white man but any foreigner, especially one who spoke the type of

halting and hesitant Creole that my brothers and I sometimes spoke with our parents. "Sa blan an di?" in our house
meant "I can't hear you. What did you say?"

My father, however, had heard me clearly.

"Grandchild," he said to my mother, while giving me a
sideways high five.

"Oh, I knew you were pregnant," my mother said, clap-
ping her short, wide hands together. "I saw it in a dream."

"More like a fantasy," my father said. "A wish."

"It was a dream," my mother said, turning to me. "I saw you
holding a baby and no one was asking you whose it was."

The rest of the ride was spent on advice that both my parents would repeat throughout my pregnancy. My mother told
me to see a doctor as soon as possible. My father ordered me
to stop traveling, get plenty of rest and try to relax.

On the curb at the airport, my father got out of the car
to hug me. He was breathing hard when he reached down to
touch my still-flat belly.

"Don't make her sad," my mother said in a way that was
partly brusque and partly playful, which was how she often
spoke. "She's going to be on that plane alone."

"It's not a private plane, is it?" my father teased, even while
trying to catch his breath.

Not wanting him to stand much longer, I gave each of my
parents a hug, then grabbed my luggage and rushed away.
From the airport lobby, I saw my father slowly slide behind
the wheel and lower his head to cough and cough and
cough. Sometimes when he coughed really hard, tears would

stream down his face that he would not even notice. Now I could see my mother reaching over and wiping his face with her palm. A strapping policeman walked up to my father's car and motioned for him to move. As the other passengers walked to the check-in lines, I watched my father, still out of breath, drive away.

Heartstrings, Shoestrings

My father quit school in 1954 at age nineteen to start an apprenticeship with a neighborhood tailor. Not just an ordinary tailor, but a man whose small at-home workshop turned out hundreds of unisex children's shirts made with the cheapest cloth, thread and labor—apprentices—available. My father was expected to sew two dozen little shirts each day. The shirts were then sold to vendors who resold them all over Haiti.

Papa's share of the profit was about five pennies per shirt. He quit after six months once he'd saved and borrowed enough money to buy his own sewing machine. He then began working for himself, selling directly to the vendors. That is, until the 1960s, when used clothes from the United States, which were called "Kennedys" because they were sent to Haiti during the Kennedy administration, became readily available.

One afternoon, my father was looking for another job when he stopped by the fabric shop where my uncle Joseph worked. He had become a regular customer there and was on good terms with the boss, who told him about an Italian émigré who'd just opened a shoe store on Grand Rue and was looking for a salesman. My father ran over to the store and, on the recommendation of my uncle's boss, was hired on the spot.

My father's new boss was always covered in jewelry. In addition to a gold necklace as thick as his belt, he wore an equally fat bracelet and two large gold rings on each hand.

"If men wore earrings back then," my father used to say, "he'd have worn four."

But the boss's personal extravagance belied what he would pay my father. His salary was modest, less than the equivalent of twenty U.S. dollars a month, with the possibility of a commission on sales of more than three pairs of shoes.

Having worked nonstop both as an apprentice and for himself, my father thought his new job would be a breeze. All he had to do was talk people into buying something they needed anyway.

The store carried shoes in many styles and price ranges. Men's shoes, women's shoes, rubber shoes, plastic shoes—and the most expensive of all, leather shoes. He was told to emphasize that all the shoes, like the owner of the shop, were from Italy.

"Otherwise you can get any street corner cordonier to make you a pair of shoes," the boss encouraged him to tell the customers.

But of course very few of the shoes were actually from Italy. The rest, he discovered, came from the United States via Puerto Rico.

Every once in a while, my uncle would recommend to his growing congregation that they buy their shoes from my father. Papa, in turn, convinced his boss to offer special discounts to my uncle's parishioners by reminding him that church people were less likely to use birth control, which meant many more potential customers.

That period in my father's life, the early sixties, was also shadowed by much larger events. Papa Doc Duvalier, who'd followed Daniel Fignolé into the presidential palace, refused to step down or allow new elections, despite a growing dissatisfaction with his increasingly repressive methods of imprisoning and publicly executing his enemies. Instead he had created a countrywide militia called the Tonton Macoutes, a battalion of brutal men and women aggressively recruited from the country's urban and rural poor. Upon joining the Macoutes, the recruits received an identification card, which showed their allegiance to Papa Doc Duvalier, an indigo denim uniform, a .38 and the privilege of doing whatever they wanted.

My father recalled how some macoutes would walk into the shoe store, ask for the best shoes and simply grab them and walk away. He couldn't protest or run after them or he might risk being shot.

After losing too many shoes, his boss came up with a solution. He ordered a large number of third-rate, non-leather shoes that looked like the real thing. Most of the macoutes who walked in wanting to steal shoes either didn't care or couldn't tell the difference anyway. If they asked to try on a pair of shoes, my father was to let them try on only the three-dollar shoes.

Papa would always get a knot in his stomach when a macoute asked him if there were other shoes. He would try not to shake as he replied, "Non," all the while bending and massaging the cheap shoes to make them appear more supple. In the end, it was this experience of bending shoes all day and worrying about being shot that started him thinking about leaving Haiti.

My parents tell slightly differently the story of how they met in 1962, when they were both twenty-seven years old. In my mother's version, they met in a Bel Air grocery store owned by one of my mother's older sisters and where she often went to help out. Back then my mother was slender, beautiful, in a brooding, melancholy kind of way, and painfully shy. One day my father walked into the tiny, dimly lit shop, where my mother greeted him with a smile at the door. A few days later she just happened to visit the shoe store on Grand Rue to buy a pair of shoes. He helped her try on a few women's shoes, none of which fit. She thanked him and left the store.

My father has no recollection of the first meeting at the grocery store. He simply remembers her walking into the shoe store, too shy to even look up from her dusty old sandals. He wanted to keep her in the store as long as possible, so he gave her shoes to try on that he knew wouldn't fit her. Finally when, frustrated, she walked out of the store, he followed her home.

They were married three years later.

Before my mother came along, Uncle Joseph wanted my father to marry Tante Denise's sister Léone, who, though she was five years younger than Tante Denise, looked like her twin. They were nearly identical, except Léone dressed more casually than Tante Denise, for whom being the pastor's wife meant never leaving the house without her matching hat and gloves and one of her many shoulder-length wigs, which she preferred to her own shortly cropped hair. The fact that Tante Denise made her own clothes and could buy cloth at a discount from my uncle's fabric shop made it easy for her to maintain her consistently elegant attire. Léone lacked the means and interest and thus always looked like the twin who, though just as pretty, had been abandoned at birth. Though Léone loved my father, he wasn't interested in her.

Besides, as he told me one night during that visit after his diagnosis, when we happened to stumble on the bride-capture musical *Seven Brides for Seven Brothers*, which he thought was about seven brothers marrying seven sisters, "It's not as if your uncle and I were Cain and Abel and there was no one else in the world to marry."

After my parents married, they moved into a small house in an increasingly packed section of Bel Air. The cement floor of their two-room rental was the same drab color as the walls. There were no windows or jalousies, just some diamond-shaped openings in the concrete, which let in some air and also plenty of water when it rained. My mother decorated the best she could, draping the walls with wide ruffled curtains she made herself. They wanted to have children right away, but couldn't conceive, prompting my uncle and Tante Denise to constantly request prayers for them at church.

My parents were about to celebrate their fourth wedding anniversary when I was born, in 1969. Twenty months later,

Bob followed. After Bob and I were born, my father started sewing again when he came home from the shoe store. My mother joined him in making school uniforms and tiny flags for schoolchildren to wave on Flag Day.

One afternoon before closing the shoe store, my father was talking to his boss about the boss's son, who was soon leaving for vacation in New York.

"You think I can get a visa?" my father asked.

Then, as now, leaving often seemed like the only answer, especially if one was sick like my uncle or poor like my father, or desperate, like both.

My father's boss offered to write him a letter of support for his application.

Because he had a job, a wife and two children as incentives to return to Haiti, my father was granted a one-month tourist visa. But he had no intention of coming back.

I have no memory of my father's departure, or of anything that preceded it. Uncle Joseph and Tante Denise's adopted daughter, Marie Micheline, liked to tell me how the year before my father left, he would often buy a small pack of butter cookies on his way home from work in the evening, which he intended to give me. I didn't like the cookies. But my face would light up when I saw them, and I'd laugh and laugh when he'd give me one and I'd return it to him only to hoot even more when he popped it in his mouth.

I've since discovered that children who spend their childhood without their parents love to hear stories like this, which they can embellish and expand as they wish. These types of anecdotes momentarily put our minds at ease, assuring us that we were indeed loved by the parent who left. Unfortunately, I wasn't told many stories like that. What I did often hear about was the future, an undetermined time when my father would send for my mother, Bob and me.

Once my father was gone, Uncle Joseph would stop by every now and then to see us after work, and of course my mother, Bob and I continued to attend services at his church. Fiercely independent and too proud to seek his involvement or ask for loans when the monthly allowance my father sent her ran out, my mother continued my father's work, sewing school uniforms and flags. One Sunday morning when she had no money at all, my mother dropped us on my uncle's lap after church so we could have a proper Sunday meal with him and Tante Denise.

"One day this will stop," my mother told him. Then she ran home, crying.

Two years after my father left, when I was four and Bob was two, the one-month tourist visa that my mother had applied and been rejected for several times was finally approved. When it came time for her to leave, we drove with her—Tante Denise, Uncle Joseph and Bob and me—to the airport. Bob sat on my mother's lap in the backseat and I sat next to her with my head leaning against her arm.

In the airport, at the gate, my mother's eyes welled with tears as she handed Bob over to Tante Denise, who quickly removed her gloves to receive him in her arms. Back then Tante Denise rarely removed her gloves in public, so the very careful gesture, her removing her gloves and patting her

wig slightly with her well-manicured fingers, seemed to me
to indicate that something big was going to happen. I didn't
know exactly when the word had come that my mother
could leave, but I should have suspected something. All that
week, my mother had been sewing me dresses: long ones
with large bows and elaborate collars, short ones in carnation prints and others with pink lace ruffles. By the end of the
week I had ten dresses in total, most of them too big for me,
so that, I realized now, I could wear them in the future, while
she was gone. She had even made me a matching version of
the plain white cotton dress that we were both wearing at
the airport, a dress that resembled the kind of modest frock
one might wear to be immersed in water at an adult baptism
at my uncle Joseph's church. It was all making sense. She had
also bought Bob three brand-new suits, two of them with
short pants and one large one with long pants. She had given
away the light blue unopened sheet set she kept under her
bed for a sick day to Marie Micheline and her ceramic pitch-
ers to Tante Denise. But she hadn't moved our things from
our house. Our beds? Our clothes? And a treasured birthday
gift from my uncle, a copy of Ludwig Bemelman's *Madeleine*.
These things, were they even now being moved to Uncle
Joseph and Tante Denise's house?

When it was time for my mother to board the plane, I
wrapped my arms around her stockinged legs to keep her
feet from moving. She leaned down and unballed my fists as
Uncle Joseph tugged at the back of my dress, grabbing both
my hands, peeling me off of her.

"Kalm," he said. "Calm yourself." And for a moment his
voice, deep, firm, did pacify me. After all, it seemed that he

and Tante Denise would now be in charge of us. They would be our parents. But what if our mother went away and never came back? Just like our father.

Panicked, I leaped out of Uncle Joseph's arms and ran right to my mother, pressing my face against her legs. I pushed him back as he tried to grab me again.

Having run from Tante Denise, Bob was also on the floor pounding his tiny fists against the cold tiles, bawling. His face was covered with some phlegm he had spit up. Answering a final boarding call, my mother hurried away, her tear-soaked face buried in her hands. She couldn't bear to look back.

We're All Dying

My mother was right about my plane ride to Miami that July 2004. It was going to be the most lonesome of my life.

After checking in and clearing security, I called my husband from the airport gate.

"I can't wait to see you *both*," he said in his unwaveringly cheerful voice.

Soon after I hung up, I learned that the flight would be delayed five hours. We wouldn't leave until eight p.m. The fluttering in my stomach, no longer mysterious, continued. It was a presence now, one to which I could assign all kinds of deeds and traits, a little baby sleeping, waking, doing cartwheels.

At that stage of the pregnancy, the baby was most likely an inch long, a tiny tadpole with a yet undeveloped heart and brain and only micro bumps for arms and legs, but he/she was already the only person, besides my dying father, who was constantly on my mind.

I called my father's cell phone to tell him I was going to be delayed. Perhaps if he wasn't too far from the airport, he could come back and get me.

He didn't answer. Was something wrong? Wrong was now the norm. Did something even worse happen? I would ask myself that question each time I called him and the phone wasn't picked up. Was he in a car crash? Was he dead?

I kept calling the house until my mother answered.

"He just dropped me off," she said, dragging her words.

"He's not answering the phone," I said.

"You know him. He probably forgot to charge it."

My father was at the car service office when he finally picked up his cell phone.

"I thought you'd left," he said.

There were times when he was relaxed and well rested that he didn't sound ill at all. As he grew sicker, I'd have to look for hints in his tone to judge for myself when he wasn't doing well.

"Should I come and get you?" he asked.

Not wanting him to overextend himself, I said, "I should probably stay in case the plane leaves sooner than expected. I just wanted you to know."

"Call me again before you take off," he said.

I had several hours left, so I speed-walked the terminals while I called my brothers to tell them the news. Bob had just left my parents' house, where he'd been visiting with my mother.

"Mom doesn't like the way you told them," he said, confirming my suspicion.

I called my mother again. After all, I reasoned, what if the plane crashed when I finally got on and I lost forever my chance to tell her I was sorry?

"Manman, eskize m, I'm sorry." Perhaps it was the combined thrill and sorrow stirred up by both the pregnancy and my father's illness, but I wanted her never to be angry with me again.

Next, I called my brother Karl at work.

"Welcome to my world," he said. I could almost see him grinning as he shuffled some papers back and forth on his desk. "You'll never be on time for anything again. And sleeping in? Forget it."

Those caveats were now a link between us. Oldest sister and baby brother, we could now discuss not just our parents but our kids.

When I called my brother Kelly, he remembered a conversation we'd had when I was a senior in high school, when I'd declared that my greatest dream in life was to be a childless spinster so I could have total freedom to write my books.

"Now the married spinster is pregnant." He laughed.

Announcing my pregnancy kept me from talking about my father, at least for a while. Walking through the terminal, I called a few friends, people I didn't want to wait the safe twelve weeks to tell. However I told only two of them the flip side of my news, that my father was dying. One, who knew my father well, became angry with me for accepting the doctor's prognosis so easily.

"What does the doctor know?" she shouted.

"He did tests," I said. "And my father knows too."

"Listen to me," she interrupted. "Screw the doctor. We're all dying. Some of us might fall in the shower and hit our heads. Some of us might get hit by a bus. Some of us might get struck by lightning. Some of us might have diseases we don't even know about. We're all dying."

Of course this had also crossed my mind. Maybe it was in the elevator on the way down from Dr. Padman's office or at the table at the family meeting or maybe it was in the car sitting between my mother and father on the drive to the airport, or some point in between, but I too had told myself the same thing. I had heard it before. From my uncle. "Maybe we're all dying, one breath at a time."

Good-bye

It's difficult not to idealize the brave face my uncle might have put on his suffering after his radical laryngectomy in 1978, even if what appeared to be bravery was simply an attempt at shielding his pain from others. However, it seemed to me, at nine years old, that my uncle was adapting well to his larynx operation. Even after he could no longer speak, he continued an early-morning routine of playing an old Berlitz record and mouthing a few English phrases while shaving.

"Good morning," a bubbly, youthful-sounding female voice would proclaim from a scratchy LP on a turntable at his bedside.

"Good evening," she'd continue.

Then she'd plunge ahead to "Good-bye."

Her good-bye contained none of the sadness the word implied. It was the type of good-bye one was likely to hear after a lively party, not the send-off that preceded a long absence or a death. Before my uncle's operation, he'd attempted to match her cheerfulness in his repetition. After the operation, he simply tried to mouth the joyful greetings and out-of-context phrases.

Eventually, it wasn't as difficult for my uncle to communicate as I'd expected. For those who knew how to read, he'd write notes explaining complicated or elaborate thoughts. The rest of the time, he used facial expressions and hand gestures. Pointing to his eyes, for example, meant look. Tugging at his ears meant listen. Pulling his hands apart meant open. Pushing them together meant close. Slapping his palm against his forehead meant he'd forgotten or overlooked something.

While my uncle was not the only mute person in Bel Air—there was a boy who was born voiceless and an old woman who'd suffered a stroke—he was the only one with a tracheotomy hole in his neck. People were so curious about the hole that they kept their eyes on it throughout entire one-way conversations with him. I too was intrigued by this narrow abyss that seemed to lead deep into his body. A perfect circle, it was salmon pink like our house and convulsed outward when he sneezed.

In their curiosity some of our neighbors were cruel. I remember once walking out of our house with my uncle and hearing a young boy call out "kou kav" or cave neck. Hearing this, the boy's mother pointed at my uncle and laughed. Her laugh was more like a self-conscious snigger than a taunt. There was almost fear in it.

I'd often seen parents warn their children not to stare at

the disabled or point at the infirm. "You mustn't gawk or your eyes will seal shut. If you point, your fingers will fall off," my own mother might have told me once or twice before she left.

The boy's mother was laughing as though she'd been told all this yet still couldn't help herself. Maybe she'd been laughing before we came by, was embarrassed that we caught her at it. Perhaps a comedy show was playing on the radio inside her house that only she and her son could hear. Still, as we walked past them, my uncle, dressed in his usual dark suit and tie, gripped my hand tightly. His body stiffened, but he held his head high and pretended not to notice.

Back then, all I could think to do was imagine a wall around him, a roaming fortress that would follow him everywhere he went and shield him from derision. This fortress, cloud-cloaked in cotton candy pink, followed us that day as I walked with him to the bank to deposit the money my parents had wired him through a money transfer service for our school fees and other expenses.

One altered facet of my uncle's post-operation life was that he didn't like to go too many places by himself. Whenever he had to make a deposit at the bank or had school business at the Education Ministry, he would wait for either me or his grandson, Maxo's son, Nick, to come back from school and take one of us with him. That way if he wasn't able to make himself understood, either with his gestures or with his sometimes indecipherable handwriting, then one of us would *interpret* him.

Our reward was the relief in the banker's or the clerk's eyes when he realized how much longer the transaction with my uncle would have taken had one or both of us not been there, how many eyes might have been needed to survey the requests in his notes, how many attempts at reading the lips before coming up with some possibilities, to which my uncle would vigorously shake his head no or nod in agreement. My uncle would be appreciative too when we'd get something right. He would break into a purposely controlled grin, one designed to conceal his false teeth. His grin would have been a thunderous "Yes!" had he been able to speak, a shout to the heavens if he could have managed it.

We got to the bank at a time when it was nearly empty. My uncle walked up to a young woman who was sitting behind her desk, talking on the phone. She hung up and motioned for us to sit down.

The air-conditioning was on full blast, filling the place with a chilled perfumed air. My uncle handed her an envelope with some bills and his passbook in it. She pulled out the bills and counted them, laying each out in front of her.

Sometimes visits like this one required no conversation or any other type of exchange that might reveal my uncle's condition. For all the woman knew, he might have been shy or ill at ease. He had been served before at that bank, but not by her. She didn't know him.

When she was done counting the money, she spoke a number out loud, to which my uncle agreed with a nod. She then typed the amount in his passbook. And just as my uncle's shoulders dropped, the equivalent for him of a sigh of relief, and just as he might have been thinking he would no longer need Nick or myself to accompany him to that particular woman at that particular bank, the woman leaned forward and asked, "Ta fille?" Your daughter?

My uncle nodded, the same blissful nod he used to indicate agreement when something was suddenly clear to him. He smiled broadly, while patting my tightly plaited hair.

On the sidewalk outside the bank was a man selling grated ice sweetened with syrup, a childhood delight called fresko. On the man's wobbly patchwork cart was a block of transparent ice half buried in sawdust and surrounded by a line of colorful bottles. My eyes followed the man's shriveled hands as he carefully tapped his grater against the ice, just as he always did, to tempt us. My uncle motioned for him to come and the cart's rubber wheels screeched against the sidewalk as he moved toward us.

"What flavor?" the fresko seller asked, pointing to the half-full bottles glittering red, blue, yellow and green in the sun. I pointed to the beige bottle. Coconut! I had tried most of the other flavors, including mint and cherry, my other favorites.

Because we were regular customers, the vendor poured me an especially generous amount. I twirled my tongue around the icy fresko until the inside of my cheeks numbed. My uncle was unable to resist and gestured for a fresko too, coconut-flavored like mine. By the time I'd finished my own, nearly three-quarters of his would be left, and reaching down to remove the empty paper cone from my hand, he would give me the rest of his.

On the way home, we passed rows and rows of used-book sellers whose yellowed and stained books were lined up in squares on the pavement and behind ropes on carts across from the national cathedral. Standing before a young man with more children's books than any other kind, my uncle asked me to choose one as a gift for myself. Leaning down, I picked a book that looked familiar, a book I'd owned before. It had a nun on the cover and on one side of her were eleven little girls in raincoats and on the other, having the luxury of an entire hand to herself, a little girl who was dressed exactly the same as the others but stood apart somehow. The little girl's name was Madeleine.

I picked up the book, as though picking up Madeleine herself, and quickly pressed it against my chest even as my uncle paid the seller. Unlike my first copy, which was brand-new and smelled of newly printed ink, this one smelled musty and ancient. My uncle didn't have a chance to look at it long enough to see that he had bought it for me before, as a birthday gift when I was four years old. In my family, we did not have birthday parties and a gift on one's birthday was not a given. Actually that first book was the only birthday gift I'd ever received from my uncle, who, perhaps knowing that that would be the last birthday I'd be spending with my mother for some time, had unceremoniously given it to her to pass on to me. The book had disappeared with my things when they'd been moved from our place to Uncle Joseph and Tante Denise's. But, fearing that he would think me careless, I'd never said a thing. Now as we walked the short distance home, I couldn't wait to climb into bed and have another visit with my old friend Madeleine, who, like me, now lived in an old house with other children. And though there were not twelve of us, there could have been, breaking our bread and brushing our teeth and going to bed smiling at the good and frowning at the bad and sometimes being very sad.

After his operation, so that things could run smoothly, my uncle hired a principal for the school and two associate pastors to manage his church. Still, there were times when it was painfully clear how much he missed the full participation his voice allowed him. This would be most obvious to me when he would skip an evening service and sit motionless in the darkest corner of the front gallery and while staring blankly ahead listen to Granmè Melina telling her folktales.

Tante Denise's mother, Granmè Melina, was probably a centenarian when she came to live with us in 1979. Like many rural Haitians of her generation, she didn't have a birth certificate and could only vaguely recall, as she'd been told by her parents, that she was born when a man named Canal Boisrond was president of Haiti. Boisrond's three-year rule, from July 1876 to July 1879, put Granmè Melina's age at somewhere between ninety-seven and one hundred years.

Illness had brought Granmè Melina from the mountains of Léogâne, where she'd been living since her daughter had moved to Port-au-Prince with Uncle Joseph. Ravaged by arthritis, both her pale, liver-spotted hands were curled into clawlike grips, making it impossible for her to do anything for herself. She spent most of her days sitting on the front gallery watching people go by. But as soon as the sun went down, she would be at the center of things as she livened up and told stories. The neighborhood children rushed through their dinner and hastened to learn the next day's lessons so they could sit on the steps beneath Granmè Melina's rocking chair and listen to her tales.

One of the stories she told most often was the Rapunzel-like tale of a beautiful young girl whose mother, fearful that she might be abducted by passersby, locked her inside a small but pretty little house by the side of the road while the mother worked in the fields until dusk. Every evening after a hard day's work, the mother would stand outside the little house and sing a simple song, which would signal to the daughter to open the door and let her mother come inside. After observing this for many weeks, a huge, deadly serpent waited until the mother was at work in the fields and then, hoping to trick the girl into coming out, slithered to her doorstep and tried to imitate her mother's song. But the serpent hissed too loudly, so the daughter could clearly tell that it was not her mother. She did not open the door, and the serpent went away and waited for another day. When the girl's mother came home later that day from the fields, the mother sang the song and the girl joyfully opened the door to the little house, letting her mother in.

Granmè Melina's voice would grow shrill with excitement from the dangers that might lie ahead for this young girl, who was, after all, our representative in the story, the one from whose choices we were meant to extract our lesson.

The next day, after the mother left for her work in the fields, the serpent returned to the girl's doorstep and once again tried to sing the mother's song. This time the serpent hissed too softly, so the daughter knew not to open the door. So the serpent went away, to wait for another day.

Granmè Melina's stories didn't always have happy end-
ings. One day, it occurred to the serpent that he could simply kill the mother and force the girl to come outside. And
so he killed her, leaving the girl all alone in the world. Still
the girl never left her little house, preferring instead to die
fresh and pure alone inside rather than risk facing the snake
outside.

Those nights, sitting at Granmè Melina's feet with the
other children and listening to her often frightening stories,
I would close my eyes and imagine it was my mother, who
never cared for such tales, telling me one of them. One night,
after Granmè Melina had received a group of children on the
porch, she complained of achy joints and asked Tante Denise to massage her body with camphor and castor oil before
bed. Propping her up against a mound of pillows, Tante Denise, who'd recently developed diabetes and was starting to
look a bit sluggish and a lot less youthful herself, asked her
niece Liline to slip Granmè Melina's nightgown over her
head. Liline's father, Tante Denise's youngest brother, Linoir,
had left Léogâne the year before to work as a cane cutter in
the Dominican Republic. Liline's mother had six other children to look after and very little money with which to do it,
so Linoir asked Tante Denise to look after Liline until he
came back. Like Marie Micheline, Bob, Nick and me, Liline
was yet another child that Uncle Joseph and Tante Denise
had not been able to turn away.

Liline and I shared a metal bunk bed across the room from
Granmè Melina. Thankfully Granmè Melina's fragrant poul-
tices and rubdowns would overpower the stench of urine ris-

ing from Liline's bottom bunk. At ten, Liline was still wetting her bed, always explaining when she was scolded by Tante Denise that she had dreamed herself peeing in a latrine when she'd soaked her mattress. I don't know how it was decided that Liline and I should share a room with Granmè Melina, but we liked having her all to ourselves those nights when she'd send everyone home but still had more stories in her before she fell asleep.

That evening, while Tante Denise dabbed Granmè Melina's wrinkled forehead with camphor and wrapped a scarf around her plaited cotton-white hair, Granmè Melina told us the story of the singing mother, the shut-in daughter and the snake, a story I thought was meant only to scare the neighborhood children. But I see now that the story was more about Granmè Melina than anyone. She was the daughter, locked inside a cocoon of sickness and old age while death pleaded to be let in somehow. That night, Granmè Melina didn't finish the story, slipping into an abruptly sound sleep. Edging closer to the kerosene lamp that served as Granmè Melina's night-light, I leafed through my *Madeleine*, which managed to make even sickness—in Madeleine's case it was appendicitis—seem like a lot of fun.

The next morning, a Saturday, my brother Bob came to wake me to go out and play with him. Bob was then nine and small for his age. A skinny, accident-prone little kid, he once had to be taken to the neighborhood clinic two times in one day, one for a tetanus shot after he stepped on a rusty nail walking barefoot outside and the other for sticking a wad of cotton too far up his nose. Bob was, as always, with Maxo's son, Nick, who was ten, like Liline and me. Nick's parents had separated soon after Nick was born, his mother leaving for Canada when his father moved to New York.

Nick was carrying a small tray with a piece of bread and a thermos full of coffee. Walking to his great-grandmother's bed, he lowered the tray and placed it on a flat surface at her feet.

"She's still sleeping?" Nick looked down at her face. It was paler than usual, wizened and pitted. Her lips were puckered and her jaws fastened tightly as though wired together. The sheet was raised over her chest in the same place Tante Denise had carefully tucked it the night before.

I checked beneath her cot. Her chamber pot was empty. She'd been unusually quiet throughout the night, I told the boys, never waking up to pee.

"I thought she asked for coffee," Nick said. "Or did Manman [as he now called his grandmother] just send it?"

Suddenly it occurred to me that she might be dead. I had seen lots of dead bodies, not in their beds at home but at viewings and funerals at my uncle's church.

Before my uncle's operation, a big part of his job was to eulogize the dead. And even after his operation, he faithfully attended all church funerals, and believing that children shouldn't be shielded from either the idea or the reality of death, he often brought Nick, Bob and me with him. So the sight of a corpse was not new to us. But the task of identifying one, recognizing the transition from the living to the dead, was.

"Let's hold a mirror to her nose," Bob suggested.

Had he heard about someone doing this? Had he seen it in one of the comic books he and Nick were always reading?

He ran out of the room and came back with one of Tante Denise's pocketbook mirrors. When he lowered the mirror to Granmè Melina's nose, the glass remained unchanged. There was no mist, no fog. Granmè Melina was not breathing.

"Check her eyes," Nick suggested.

Moving his face closer to Granmè Melina's, Bob pulled back one of her eyelids. Leaning in, I saw what looked like a brown marble with bright red veins wrapped around it.

"Li mouri," he said calmly. She's dead.

"Are you sure?" Nick asked.

The eyelid did not snap back by itself, so Bob had to lower it with the same index finger with which he'd raised it. By then we were all sure.

Until his operation, a death meant an eloquent homily from my uncle, a sermon that echoed my friend's declaration that indeed, every day, we are all dying.

"Death is a journey we embark on from the moment we are born," he'd say. "An hourglass is turned and the sand starts to slip in a different direction as soon as we emerge from our mother's womb. Thank God those around us are too blinded by joy then to realize it. Otherwise there would be weeping at births as well. But if we weep at a death, it's because we do not understand death. If we saw death as another kind of birth, just as the Gospel exhorts us to, we wouldn't weep, but rejoice, just as we do at the birth of a child."

My uncle's funeral homilies had rarely varied from this. Still, during Granmè Melina's funeral, as he sat quietly in his usual seat at the altar, he might have had more personal words in mind for his mother-in-law. For at some point during the service, when one of the associate pastors was announced, my uncle got up from his seat and raced to the pulpit.

Sitting in the front pew with her sister Léone and two of her brothers, Tante Denise moved from side to side, shifting her weight uneasily. Unlike Léone, who wore a plain, short-sleeved, black cotton dress, Tante Denise wore a black lace dress with matching gloves and veil.

Nick leaned over and whispered to Bob and me, "What's Papa"—as he called his grandfather—"doing?" We were sitting in the second row, behind Tante Denise, who turned back and gave us a scolding glance as Uncle Joseph stood motionless behind the pulpit. Tante Denise wasn't one to coddle children and could have easily pulled any one of us aside for a spanking, even in the middle of her own mother's funeral service.

Tante Denise turned her eyes back to the front of the church and along with the entire congregation was once again looking up at my uncle. Had he forgotten that he couldn't speak? Should they expect some kind of miracle? But standing there as though stunned into silence, his face sullen, his eyes circling the room—Granmè Melina's death perhaps a reminder of how close he himself had come to dying—he appeared a lot more distressed than the rest of the mourners. Reaching for the microphone, he unhinged it from its stand and raised it to his lips. He opened his mouth and just as he did every morning along with his Berlitz record, he mouthed one word: "Good-bye."

A few gasps rose from the congregation, perhaps from people who thought they heard the same breathy murmur that those of us who were used to reading his lips and speaking for him often thought we heard. This, he seemed to want to say, was not like all the other funerals he'd attended, where he wished he'd been able to speak but couldn't: those of the kids who died from microbes and viruses in infancy, the adolescents crushed by careless drivers on their way to or from school, the women who fell to malaria or typhoid fever or tuberculosis, the men who were beaten or shot to death by the henchmen of François Duvalier and later after his death in 1971, his replacement, son Jean-Claude. This was a woman, an old woman, who had traveled a long way from home and who had lived a *long* life. He too was hoping to live a long life. He had traded his voice for a cure. But now he couldn't even properly say good-bye.

Giving Birth

Marie Micheline, Uncle Joseph and Tante Denise's adopted daughter, was secretly pregnant in 1974, the year I turned five and she twenty-two. Wiry and slight, she was nevertheless able to hide her growing belly for nearly twenty-eight weeks, until the morning she overslept and didn't wake up for an important nursing school exam.

When Tante Denise went to rouse her, she found her in her room, lying on her back, her stretched-out navel pointing straight up at the ceiling.

"Joseph Nosius!" Tante Denise cried out for my uncle, as though both she and Marie were in mortal danger.

Uncle Joseph was slow in coming, but Liline and I ran to Marie Micheline's bedside. Liline and I both adored Marie Micheline because she was kind and pretty. But above all because of this: even though she was much older than us, she occasionally took time to ask us to her room or to sit down next to us at a meal and whisper in our ear a story that proved how much our absent parents loved us. Mine was the story of the butter cookies, which she told me over and over again. I don't know what the details of Liline's story were, but it had something to do with her father leaving her with us.

"He loved you so much," she would say out loud at the end of the story, "he left you with us."

With Tante Denise panting over her, Marie Micheline stirred and tried to rub the sleep out of her eyes. Her short hair was curled in tight sponge rollers and wrapped in the thick dark web of a fishnet. When she removed her hands from her eyes she seemed unsure of what we were all doing there.

"You can't stay in this house now." Tante Denise grabbed her by the shoulder and shook her. "Your father's a pastor. How is it going to look if his daughter is pregnant without the benefit of marriage?"

Of course, Tante Denise herself had been pregnant and had given birth to Maxo without the benefit of a church ceremony. But her status back then had been different. Hers had been, even if not a religious marriage, a common-law one. She was in love with and living with her man and she was not yet in the church.

Marie Micheline looked down at her stomach, quickly lowered the nightgown and raised the sheet that had slipped off her body during the night. She did not immediately look up as Uncle Joseph at last walked into the room. He still had his crisp and muted voice then and lowered it even more to signal calm.

Sitting at the foot of the bed, he gently stroked Marie Micheline's covered feet.

"What's the matter?" he asked.

Marie Micheline looked into his eyes. I want to understand, they seemed to say. Her long, narrow face, which sometimes looked as smooth and peaceful as a plastic doll's, crumpled into sobs.

"She's pregnant," Tante Denise yelled, pulling the sheet and nightgown aside to show him Marie Micheline's stomach.

My uncle gasped at the sight. Marie Micheline's belly was small but heavily veined. Still it looked as though it might soon creep up and swallow the space occupied by her breasts.

"How many months?" he asked.

"Seven," Marie Micheline answered, now cradling the belly between her hands. She purposely kept her eyes down, doing her best not to look at a fuming Tante Denise.

"What have we ever done to you?" Tante Denise cried out in a strained, high-pitched voice. "Haven't we taken care of you from the time you were a baby?"

Marie Micheline sat up and lowered her feet off the bed.

"I knew it," she shouted. "I knew you'd act like this. I'm pregnant, not ungrateful."

My uncle raised his hands, signaling for them to quiet down. Then he motioned for Liline and me to leave the room.

"Who's the father?" we heard him ask as we left.

Liline and I didn't wander too far from the doorway. The father, Marie Micheline stammered, was Jean Pradel, the oldest of five brothers who lived across the alley from us. Jean had four brothers, our neighbors often whispered, because his mother had been in pursuit of a girl.

The Pradel boys were handsome young men, well built and, thanks to the financial gains from their mother's ice and soda shop and their father's tailoring business, well educated. Their father was somber and fussy and was always well groomed, spending the days when he wasn't working in a rocking chair on his immaculate front porch.

"Does Jean know he's the father?" my uncle asked. "Will he deny it and humiliate us? Or will he own up to it like a man?"

"I don't know," Marie Micheline answered.

"Get up and get dressed," my uncle said. "We're going to have a visit with Monsieur and Madame Pradel."

Liline and I scattered as they left Marie Micheline's room and began to move toward us. While Marie Micheline dressed, Tante Denise and Uncle Joseph waited in front of her bedroom door, not saying a word to one another.

Marie Micheline came out in her too-large white nursing school uniform. Her belly was still undetectable under her clothes, but now she put less effort into hiding it, letting her body move naturally in a way that clearly showed her struggles with sluggishness and the extra weight.

Sandwiched between the only parents she'd ever known, she slowly walked toward the Pradels.

The meeting didn't last long. When they returned, we could tell by the angry look on Tante Denise's and Uncle Joseph's faces and by Marie Micheline's despondent gaze that Jean Pradel had denied being the father.

"See what you get when you lie down with pigs," Tante Denise said loud enough for the Pradels to hear as they sat huddled at a table by their front door.

"Get your things," Tante Denise told Marie Micheline. "You're going to live with one of my cousins in Léogâne. We'll send you money and food. You can come back when the baby's born."

"Let's not be rash," Uncle Joseph interjected. "We can go back and see what the boy says. He'd obviously not told his parents and was taken by surprise."

"This is women's business," Tante Denise said. "Let me take care of it."

We were not allowed to say good-bye to Marie Micheline when she left the next day. Many of our neighbors assumed she was sent abroad to join Maxo. Tante Denise did not send her to Léogâne either, but to live with Liline's mother in a distant and destitute part of town. Soon the Pradels also sent Jean to Montreal, where he had some relatives, and we never saw him again.

During the two months that Marie Micheline was gone, Uncle Joseph and Tante Denise visited her several times but never took any of us children with them. After one of the visits I overheard Tante Denise telling her sister Léone that Marie Micheline, heartbroken over Jean Pradel's rejection, had gotten married in a civil ceremony.

"Who would marry a pregnant girl?" asked Léone.

"A kind man who wants to give an abandoned child a name," Tante Denise answered proudly.

"He must want something," Léone countered.

The next piece of news was that Marie Micheline's baby was born, healthy and a girl. My uncle rented a small apartment for Marie Micheline, her new husband and the child, then he and Tante Denise went to pick them up and bring them back to Bel Air. They paid a few months' rent, then the husband was supposed to pick up the rest.

We knew little about Marie Micheline's new husband except his name, Pressoir Marol, and the fact that he was in his thirties. After my uncle had moved them into their new place, I overheard him telling one of his friends that Pressoir spoke some Spanish, which indicated that he might have spent some time working as a cane laborer or construction worker either in Cuba or in the Dominican Republic. The fact that Pressoir walked with a slight limp also hinted at the possibility of an injury acquired doing that type of work.

Marie Micheline, Pressoir and the baby, whose name was Ruth, often came to eat at the house. As she walked over from her place to ours, Marie Micheline would have to pass by the Pradels' house, where Monsieur Pradel was frequently sitting out on the porch, either pedaling at his sewing machine or watching the street.

One afternoon, Marie Micheline stopped right in front of Monsieur Pradel and waited for him to look up and acknowledge her. When he didn't, she turned the baby's tiny face toward him and said, "I'm not interested in Jean anymore, Monsieur Pradel. Wherever he is, I just want him to acknowledge his daughter."

"Don't you already have a husband?" Monsieur Pradel asked scornfully.

Dressed in the indigo denim uniform of the Tonton Macoutes, Pressoir was waiting on our front gallery, where Nick, Bob and I were playing, and he too overheard this exchange. He was wearing the macoute's signature dark reflector glasses, which completely hid his eyes. Enraged, he dashed toward Marie Micheline and grabbed her by the elbow, nearly shaking Ruth out of her grasp. Pressoir hadn't yet been assigned a gun, which is perhaps the only reason he didn't shoot both Marie Micheline and Monsieur Pradel on the spot.

"You whore, you shameless bouzen," he yelled as he pushed Marie Micheline into our house.

My uncle went to Marie Micheline's aid. By then, Ruth had woken up and was wailing.

"What's happening here?" My uncle seemed as perplexed by Ruth's distress and Marie Micheline's sobs as he was by Pressoir's menacing uniform.

"You're a macoute?" my uncle asked Pressoir, all the while shaking his head, showing his shock and disapproval.

"My wife will no longer be coming here," Pressoir said, ignoring my uncle's question. "From now on, if you want to see her and the baby, you'll have to come to us."

Tante Denise stumbled out from the kitchen and wiped the sweat from her crinkled forehead with a corner of the flowered scarf around her head.

"What are you saying?" she asked, also sobbing now. "She's our daughter. This is our grandchild."

"Just what I say," Pressoir replied. "I thought she was coming here to see you. That's not what she's doing. So she's no longer allowed to come."

Two days later, Pressoir moved Marie Micheline and Ruth out of the place my uncle had rented for them. He left word with their landlord for my aunt and uncle that he now had bullets and that Marie Micheline was forbidden to see anyone. To keep them from finding Marie Micheline and Ruth, he moved them constantly, staying with other macoutes only a few days at a time, sometimes separating them and placing Ruth in the temporary care of strangers.

My uncle eventually managed to track them down near the ocean a few miles south of Port-au-Prince and visited with them when Pressoir was away. When Pressoir heard that he'd been there, he moved them back to the outskirts of Latounèl, a small village in the mountains of Léogâne.

After two months with no word from Marie Micheline, my uncle finally learned where she was from a family friend who lived in the same area. He decided that no matter what the risks, he would go there and bring her home.

Climbing the rugged mountain trails on a borrowed mule at high noon, my uncle thought he'd never make it to the village. The mule was hiking at a steady gait, but my uncle was hot, thirsty, and covered with sweat and his head and backside ached. Still, all he could think of was seeing Marie Micheline and the baby again. He blamed himself for letting Tante Denise send her away when she was pregnant. Why hadn't he forced her to annul her marriage? He should have been more diligent, much more suspicious. Who marries a pregnant girl—as Léone had asked—even one as pretty and smart as Marie Micheline, unless there's something else behind it? In Pressoir's case, that something seemed to have been cruelty and madness.

When he reached the village, my uncle walked to the house of its highest official, the section chief, a toothless old man, who in his own starched denim uniform and dark reflector glasses reminded him of the much younger Pressoir.

"A man whose eyes you can't look into is not a man you can ever trust," his father, Granpè Nozial, had often said.

The macoutes had a synchronized look, a coarse veneer that made the thin ones seem stout, the short ones seem tall. In the end they were all equally intimidating because they represented the government. Whether it was Pressoir or this old man, each one had the power to decide whether or not my uncle lived or died, whether or not his daughter lived or died.

Fearfully putting his hand on the old man's shoulder, my uncle said, "Father, for your hair is white enough and you're old enough that I can call you father, please help me, another father, free my daughter from her bondage."

He gave the old man the equivalent of five U.S. dollars, which he wished he could get back when the old man said, "Pressoir's a real big chief now, a city macoute. None of us can cross him. Your daughter isn't the only girl he has in this condition. There are many others. Many."

"Then please, father," my uncle pleaded while trying to maintain his calm, "do me only this favor. Forget you ever saw me, but I'm not leaving without my daughter and her child."

"I won't say anything to him," the old man said as he pocketed the money. He then reluctantly gave my uncle directions to the one-room house where Marie Micheline was living.

My uncle found the house on a nearby hill, then secured a secluded grazing spot for the mule, where he too rested until dusk. As the moon started peering out of the sky, he watched Pressoir leave in full uniform, perhaps to attend a meeting.

His heart began to race. What if there was someone else in there? What if Pressoir came back? What if he failed and only made things worse for Marie and the baby?

Finally he built up enough courage to walk up the hill and into the tiny house. Marie Micheline was lying on her back on a woven banana leaf mat, which aside from a small earthen jar and a kerosene lamp was the only thing in the small shack. The limestone walls were covered with sheets of newspaper, snippets of fading bulletins that he imagined she'd read over and over again to keep herself hopeful, and calm.

"Vini," my uncle said, reaching down and pulling her up into his arms.

"Papa, is it really you?" she whispered. Now he could see that her legs were covered with pus-filled blisters, open and discolored wounds. Her gaunt face was hot and moist. She had a fever.

"He beat me. He beat me on my legs, with a broom, with fire stones when I tried to escape." She began to cry, her tears even warmer on his arm than her skin.

"Where's Ruth?" he asked.

She pointed out the door, toward another hill. The baby was with a family down the road, she whispered.

"They're good. They will give her to me," she said.

"Let's go, then." As they walked out the door, she stumbled, catching herself just in time before falling nearly flat on her face. He wrapped her body in his arms, thinking that she felt the same to him now as when her father had placed her in his arms as a baby, trusting that he would look after her, that he would always keep her from harm.

Outside, the night sky was full of stars, the kind of stars that he rarely took time to look up at and examine in the city, the way he had nearly every night when he was a boy.

"Papa," she whispered, her mouth now so close to his ears that her breath burned his lobes. "Papa, even though men cannot give birth, you just gave birth tonight. To me."

The Return

One afternoon in October 1976, when I was seven years old, Bob, Nick and I were sitting on my uncle's front gallery, memorizing, just like every other schoolchild in Haiti, our usual rote lessons for the next school day, when we saw some strange figures turn the corner from Rue Tirremasse and head down the alley toward us.

One was a man in a brown three-piece suit that looked like it was getting its first wear. He was carrying a briefcase in one hand and grasping a boy's elbow with the other. A plump woman followed with a baby in her arms. Immediately trailing them was a taxi driver and a few other young men who carried four large suitcases up to the gallery and set them at our feet.

The first thing I noticed when I looked up from their outsized, outstretched luggage was the man's smile. It was huge, cavernous, two of his top front teeth golden.

"Edwidge, it's Papa," he said, pressing that extensive smile against the side of my face. He smelled of a cologne whose fragrance I couldn't recognize, of travel and faraway places.

Was he really my father, I wondered, this thin, happy man with a thick dark beard that caressed his collarbone when he lowered his head? He kept his eyes on me, letting them wander for only a few seconds while he reached into his pocket to pay the driver and the young men who'd helped with the bags.

Until that moment, aside from the butter cookies and restrained words of his letters, my father had mostly been a feeling for me, powerful yet vague, without a real face, a real body, like the one looming over the pecan-hued little boy who was looking up at Nick, Bob and me.

"Edwidge?" My mother stepped onto the front porch, plugging the remaining hole in the circle that was now all of us.

"Come and kiss your manman," she said.

She looked heavier than I remembered, and her copper-colored skin was a few shades lighter. The baby in her arms was sleeping.

"Manman?" Bob's jaw dropped. He ran to her and planted a kiss on the first place his lips reached on her body, the woolen plaid skirt covering her legs. Balancing the baby with one arm, she reached down and with her other hand stroked his head, gently, softly, for a long time. He in turn remained glued to her skirt, burying his face deep into it as though he were crying and didn't want the rest of us to see.

I thought he had forgotten her. She'd left when he was two, the age I was when my father left, yet whatever was drawing him to her—yearning, pain, curiosity—was keeping me away from him.

"Bob." My father reached over and gently pulled him away.

Bob turned to my father's lowered face and kissed his cheek. My father was pleased, rubbing Bob's head with his palm.

"This is your brother Kelly," my father said, introducing him to the little boy by their side.

It was thanks to Kelly that our parents had been able to return to Haiti. Even though they had overstayed tourist visas, Kelly's birth in the United States had instantly made them eligible for permanent residency, which is no longer possible today.

Before things were finalized, however, they had to file the paperwork at the consulate in Port-au-Prince; only then could they petition for Bob and me to join them in New York.

"Any granmoun here?" my father asked, gently patting my shoulder with his hand.

It was late afternoon, the near-dinner hour. The water women had just filled up their buckets at the municipal tap near the Lycée Pétion and were calling out in a singsong that we sometimes listened for when our supply was low.

Dlo, dlo, dlo pou vann.

I have water for sale!

At the turn where the alley curved toward the street, Boniface, the blacksmith, was hammering an oil drum into a thin sheet of metal that he would then mold into a metal wreath to sell at the cemetery. Two of the Pradel brothers were taking turns reciting their lessons out loud in a unified refrain. Two others were playing an impromptu soccer game on their parents' front porch with an empty Carnation milk can. Their maid, a girl younger than all of them, began burning her weekly accumulation of trash, suddenly filling the alley with rank white smoke.

My parents walked inside the house to avoid the smoke. Guided by Bob and Nick, my father shut the jalousies and piled his suitcases next to the few living room chairs.

Tante Denise was cooking supper and Uncle Joseph lying down for a nap. I told Bob to go and get her, then I rushed to the room where my uncle lay curled on his side, barechested. He was startled when I shook him and thrust at him a shirt that was laid out on his night table.

"My father and mother are here," I said.

He looked at me as though I'd grown two heads. Still, he quickly got dressed and followed me.

"Frè m." My father ran into my uncle's arms.

"Why didn't you tell me you were coming?" my uncle said.

They remained attached for a while, intertwined, as if one might never release the other. Stepping away first, my father left an imprint of his wet face on the front of my uncle's shirt.

"Mesi frè m," my father said. "Thank you for looking after my children."

"Mira," my uncle said, laughing. Mira was my father's nickname, short for Miracin, his middle name. It was, I learned, what everyone called him. "These children almost look after themselves."

Tante Denise ran out of the kitchen, and though uncharacteristically joyful, she still scolded my mother with a wagging finger for not having warned her they were coming. My father asked Bob and Nick to go buy him a pack of cigarettes, and they hurried off to a street stand, happy to have so big a job to do.

"Come," my mother said, patting the chair next to hers. She smelled like coconut, which I eventually figured out came from her hair pomade. Her voice, clipped, quick, had slowly been fading from my memory. I wanted to lean over and place my head on her arm, just as I had in the back of the car the day she left, but I was too shy to do it.

The baby had woken up, his round face creased and crumpled.

"His name is Karl," she said, "and he's two months old."

Looking down at Karl, snugly cradled in our mother's arms, I couldn't help but feel envious. If she could bring him here from New York, why hadn't she been able to take Bob and me with her when she left? At the same time, I could tell from the way she stopped now and then to run her fingers over both his face and mine that she meant him to be a link between us.

"Can I hold him a little?" I asked.

Not used to holding babies then, I was shocked when she leaned over and actually placed his doughy wriggling little body in my arms.

Our extended family gathered quickly as news of my parents' arrival spread. Crowding the living room were my father's sisters, Tante Zi and Tante Tina, Tante Denise's brothers George and Bosi, Marie Micheline and two-year-old Ruth, who along with Kelly skipped and hopped and crawled between our legs. Dragging on a cigarette, my father sprinted around and beamed at everyone. Family members, including my aunts, and even strangers who saw my father during that visit tell me they'd found his charm magnetic and contagious, almost like a movie star or a politician. But then again, my father would later tell me, it was easy to be charming when you returned home on a trip that you'd been dreaming about, practicing and rehearsing in your mind for years. Even the cigarette was like a prop in a play. He was an actor playing the part of someone who wished he wasn't a factory worker or a taxi driver.

That night, between cigarettes, my father recounted New York to us.

"What does snow feel like?" Tante Denise's oldest brother, George, asked.

My father didn't talk about how cold and damp snow could be or how slippery and dangerous it could become when gelled and frozen. He didn't talk about the beauty of the individual flakes or how a few feet of them could look like a pasty rug over a lumpy bed. The only thing we have to compare it to, he simply said, was hail.

"I hear it can be just as dangerous in New York," Tante Denise's other brother, Bosi, said. "As dangerous as it can be with the macoutes here."

This led my father into two urban legends from New York's Haitian community. A woman was robbed weekly by a masked young man in the elevator of her apartment building. One day she carried a kitchen knife, which she used to stab her robber. When she removed the thief's mask, she realized it was her son. In the other story, a young man had led some school pals to five thousand dollars that his mother was hiding in her mattress and in a struggle for the money the mother had been shot.

My father told these stories as though he had seen them happen, in the elevator, in the bedroom. As he spoke, his audience gasped, in awe, in fear, in admiration of his pluck.

"New York, like today's Haiti," he said, while bouncing a tired-looking Kelly on his lap, "is a place where only the brave survive."

My father yawned, reminding us that he, my mother and Kelly and Karl had an appointment at the American consulate early the next morning. Dressing for bed, I wondered whether Bob and I would be excused from our usual sleeping arrangements—he with Nick and me with Liline—to bunk with our prodigal family. But there wasn't enough space. In one of the spare rooms, my father and Kelly were already sharing a cot so my mother and Karl could have a bed to themselves.

I waited until everyone else in the house was in bed before going in to say good night. Walking on the tips of my toes, I rapped softly on the door so I wouldn't wake the baby. My mother was already asleep with Karl at her side. Before my mother had left us, one night she and Bob had dozed off together in bed tucked tightly against each other, just as she and Karl were now. This was my first experience of nearly heart-shattering jealousy.

There was only my father to say good night to now, and Kelly, whose eyes were barely open, his super-long eyelashes batting between wakefulness and sleep. Fearing the wiry hairs on my father's prickly beard, I closed my eyes when I kissed his cheek. And even as he pulled me into his arms and poked at my ribs and tried to make me laugh, I was still certain that I would open my eyes and he'd be gone.

The next morning my parents left for the consulate at dawn. As Bob, Nick and I ate our breakfast, the house seemed strangely empty, void of their sudden, but now vital presences.

Fidgeting on the edge of his seat, Bob said, "Manman and Papa had an appointment. They'll be back."

"Be quiet," I ordered. "You don't know what you're saying."

"I know," he said. His mouth curled up and he looked like he was going to cry.

I could imagine him announcing to the other children in his class that his parents, who his classmates knew were living in New York, had come back. He didn't seem to understand that they'd not come to stay.

•

Returning from school, we found my father sitting in the living room next to my uncle, the two of them sifting through a handful of pictures from their mother's funeral. Granmè Lorvana had died soon after everyone had moved to Bel Air and was the first member of our family to be buried outside of Beauséjour. Hers was our clan's first funeral procession with hired musicians trailing her hearse as it crept toward a newly constructed city mausoleum. In their mother's funeral pictures, my father, mustached and youthful, was photographed standing next to the brand-new mausoleum with his brothers and sisters.

"Look at this one." My father held out one of the pictures to my uncle, suddenly reminding me of the way Bob and I sometimes sought my uncle's attention. For most of my father's life, my uncle had been more a parental than a fraternal figure. With twelve years between them—in his time, my uncle liked to say, a twelve-year-old was already a man—neither one of them had any memory of ever playing together. When my father was born, my uncle had been too busy studying, working, and doing his best to help look after the family.

"How was school?" my uncle asked, looking up from the pictures at Bob and me.

"How was it?" echoed my father.

Bob walked over and, ignoring my uncle completely, jumped on my father's lap.

"Okay, I'm not going to forget this," teased my uncle.

I leaned over and kissed them both on the cheek, making sure, after my brother's slight, to kiss my uncle first. As I did this, my father reached into his pants pocket and handed Bob a fistful of American pennies. Some of the copper coins were bright and new, others older and darker. As my brother tried to balance them in his small hand, many of the pennies slipped and fell to the floor, rolling into unseen corners under the sofas and chairs.

Weeks, months after my father had left, I would find his pennies all throughout the house, in sunken corners of the living room floor, between the mattresses on the cot where he slept. Before deciding what to do with them, I would drape pieces of white paper over them and trace the outline of the man on one side, a man with a beard just like my father's.

Once they'd been granted their residency papers, my parents planned to stay another week. But they had to cut their trip short when both Kelly and Karl got sick with diarrhea. My uncle took them to the neighborhood clinic where Marie Micheline worked as the head nurse. The doctor there advised my parents to quickly take the boys back to their own doctors in the United States.

This time at the airport, my mother looked anxious as she clutched a fidgety Karl to her chest. Walking to the outdoor staircase leading to the plane, my father made Kelly wave toward the second-floor patio, where Uncle Joseph, Tante Denise and Bob and I were standing. At the airplane's entrance, my mother adjusted Karl in her arms and freed one of her hands to wave back. They hadn't told us anything. Would they be back? Would we soon be joining them? We were never told things directly, I thought even then. That would imply that we had a say when we really had none.

At the airport, I thought I might cry, throw another tantrum as I did the first time my mother left, but I didn't, and neither did Bob. We were much older now and were more accustomed to being without them than being with them. At least, I remember thinking, we had seen them again.

One Papa Happy, One Papa Sad

In 1980, four long years after my parents' visit, the American consulate wrote to my uncle requesting that Bob and I take a physical to see if we were in good enough health to travel to the United States. I was eleven years old.

Usually a physical was the last step in approving an application, so everyone began to speak to me as though I were already gone.

"In New York," Tante Denise said, "you'll have to be good and help your mother."

"In New York," Marie Micheline said, "you must write me every week so you can keep up your French."

"In New York," Nick said, "be sure to buy me a nice watch."

"In New York," Liline said, "be sure to find me a gold necklace."

I agreed to everything, of course. When I get to New York, I thought, I'll have to become a slave to fulfill all the promises I've made.

Between us and New York, however, stood a list of consulate-approved doctors and the extensive examination they were required to perform.

My uncle chose a doctor whose clinic had the feel of a transitional middle world between our parents' and ours. On the walls of his examining room were hygiene posters in Creole, French and Spanish, and diplomas and certificates from both Haitian and American universities.

The doctor was short and barrel-chested with skin the same color as his curly black hair, which he wore parted on one side. As he pushed my head back and pried open my mouth, he spoke to me in French, then repeated himself in English.

"Parce qu'il faudra bientôt apprendre l'anglais," he said. Because you'll soon have to learn English.

While Bob and my uncle looked on, he made me push out my tongue, palpated my neck for swollen glands, listened to my heart and lungs with his stethoscope, then hit my knees with a small hammer, making my legs rise involuntarily. After he'd done the same to Bob, he wrote out a referral for chest X-rays to be taken at the public hospital down the street.

The small windowless waiting room in the public hospital's radiography department was filled with many more patients than it could hold comfortably. More were already interned in the hospital and were lying on gurneys in the narrow hallway. Others were sitting on the few available chairs or on the chipped cement floor, their fractured limbs wrapped in homemade bandages and slings. Others tried to cough discreetly even as they held their chests and hid the bright red spots they'd spat into their handkerchiefs, a sure sign of tuberculosis.

When my turn came, I followed the attendant into a dark room with a giant machine. My uncle and Bob were told to wait outside, leaving me in the dark with the stranger. The spark was like a flash of lightning. The attendant came around again, this time putting me in profile.

My uncle and I waited in the hallway as Bob had his turn. Pacing back and forth, my uncle kept his head down and both his hands in his pockets. Since his surgery, hospitals made him extremely nervous.

A few days later, the doctor sent word for us to return to his office. When we entered the examining room, he was wearing a white surgical mask.

"The X-rays have returned," he said, looking only at my uncle. His voice was slightly distorted by the mask, so he raised it slightly to make sure my uncle heard him. "There's a problem."

He knew that Uncle Joseph couldn't speak and did not expect a reply.

"These children," he said, glancing momentarily at Bob and me, "appear to have tuberculosis."

My uncle raised both his eyebrows to display shock. I too was surprised. After all, we didn't have a cough that made us spit up blood. Would we now have to be quarantined, be sent to the sanatorium?

One of Liline's cousins, who was named Melina after Granmè Melina, had gotten full-blown tuberculosis at sixteen. She had visited Liline now and then, and I'd watched as she'd regularly stop whatever she was doing to double over and cough. She was eventually sent to the sanatorium and died a few weeks after her seventeenth birthday.

Sleeping on the top bunk above Liline and her, those few times she'd spent the night, I'd probably caught the tuberculosis from her and passed it on to my brother. Or maybe Bob had caught it from a kid at school, a kid who didn't even know he had it, and had passed it on to me.

"Fortunately their tuberculosis is not active," the doctor said, "but we have to treat them immediately to be sure it stays that way. The treatment will last six months."

Does that mean I'm not going to die? I wanted to ask.

My uncle's mouth narrowed into a small O. Six months of treatment meant six more months in Haiti. That would mean six more months with our uncle and aunt and our cousin and friends, but also six more months away from our parents and brothers. Just then, sitting in the doctor's old and prickly wicker chair, I was not concerned about any of that. I simply didn't want to have tuberculosis and I certainly did not want to die.

I would think back to this moment when, early in my father's illness, after a weeklong hospitalization following an emergency room visit for shortness of breath, he was quarantined at Coney Island Hospital because his skin test was positive. The doctors had not yet eliminated the possibility of tuberculosis, and all the hospital workers, along with my father's visitors, were ordered to wear surgical masks before they approached his bed in an isolated section of the ward. Perhaps recalling the horrors of tuberculosis—it was once as deadly as AIDS during the virus's early years—the specter of mortality it posed, and the fact that in Bel Air the word "pwa-trinè," or TB carrier, had often been hurled as an insult, when he was quarantined at Coney Island Hospital, my father asked my brother Karl to tell the doctors that a lot of Haitians test positive on the skin test even though they don't actually have active tuberculosis.

"I don't have this disease," he insisted. "Tell them."

"We don't have this disease," I wanted to scream that day as the doctor gave us—rather, gave my uncle—our directives.

"Even though they're not infectious, we can't be too careful," the doctor said. "They must now use their own utensils. No sharing with others."

Since we all shared meals and utensils at home, this would be a constant reminder both to us and everyone else that our bodies were hosting a potentially deadly contagion.

"They have to follow the treatment closely," the doctor continued. "They must take the pills every day or the virus will get stronger and will move to other parts of their bodies. Unless their X-rays read differently in six months, they won't be able to travel."

He wrote two prescriptions, which he handed to my uncle.

"Don't forget," he told us, looking into our faces at last. "Every morning when you take your pills, you're closer to New York."

My uncle stopped by a pharmacy on Grand Rue, where his youngest sister, Tante Zi, had a stationery stand. Surrounded by mounds of pens and notebooks, Tante Zi jumped out of her chair and instantly scooped Bob up in her arms.

Of my father's sisters, Tante Zi was the most playful. Short and plump, and at her roundest looking and feeling like a feather pillow, she liked to pull Bob and me into her arms whenever she saw us and bury her face in our necks, tickling us with the tip of her nose.

She and Bob were caught in just such an embrace when I blurted out, "You can't do that anymore."

"Why not?" She released Bob, handing him a brand-new pen and notebook to scribble in as he sat on the footstool in front of her.

"Because we have TB," I said.

She seemed stunned, looking up at my uncle for confirmation. My uncle shrugged, then slapped one hand on top of the other as if to say, "What are you going to do?"

As if to answer, Tante Zi motioned for me to come to her, and just as she always had, wrapped her arms around my neck and sweetly buried her nose in my neck.

From that day on, every morning before school, even as other children walked by and stared, my uncle would line Bob, Nick and me up on the front gallery and as Tante Denise held our ceramic cups of water—our own, which we were not allowed to share with anyone else—handed us the aspirin-like pills that were meant to cure us. Nick, it turned out, also "failed" his precautionary X-rays and had to be treated along with us. Liline, however, had tested negative.

Once the pill was in our mouths, my uncle would hand us each a large spoonful of cod-liver oil, which we were to swallow before Tante Denise would surrender the water.

Perhaps fearing that we might gag, Tante Denise would always cry out, "Fè vit, fè vit," urging us to hurry up and wash the pills down, before she took the cups back.

During our treatment, Bob developed a palm-sized rash on his back that alternately bled and scabbed over. At first the doctor, whom during our monthly checkups I began to think of as Dr. TB, told us that Bob's rash was unrelated to his medication, but then I developed an even larger lesion on my right buttock, and he was forced to admit some connection. Nick, on the other hand, completely lost his appetite, dropped eight pounds, and constantly complained of cold feet.

Thankfully the rashes, coldness and loss of appetite went away when our treatment ended six months later. After another series of X-rays, Dr. TB gave Bob and me our medical clearance to travel to the United States.

But a new problem emerged. During the six months that we were being treated, my father was laid off from the glass factory where he was working, and because both my parents and Kelly and Karl were now surviving on my mother's modest income as a textile factory worker, our application was placed on hold until my father could prove that he and my mother had enough income to provide for all of us. Just when my uncle needed them most, my father stopped writing us letters around this time. In his final note, he proposed that we try the now much cheaper call centers run by Teleco, the national telephone company.

As we waited for Papa to find another job, every Sunday afternoon my uncle, Bob and I would walk to a calling center near the fabric shop where my uncle worked, and the three of us would squeeze into a narrow telephone booth with cardboard-thin walls and try to talk with my parents. The conversations were always the same. My uncle would scribble a few notes on the small notepad he kept in his shirt pocket: instant letters that in a few sentences updated our parents on the state of our health, our schoolwork, our grades, the latest on our immigration application. I would carefully repeat my uncle's scrawled phrases, watching his lips for modifications as I went on. It was hot and cramped with the three of us in there and every once in a while my uncle would have to change places with us on the narrow bench as we passed the phone around. My parents would interrupt me now and then to make a comment or ask a question and I'd have to stop and wait for my uncle to respond before speaking again. The remaining time was for our parents to speak directly to us.

"Now tell me how you are," my mother would ask me.

"Byen," I'd answer. Fine.

On another extension, my father asked, "You're being a good girl, aren't you?"

"Wi papa," I'd answer, feeling that I had already spoken to them enough, using my uncle's words.

"I've found a job," my father announced one Sunday afternoon.

"Bravo!" my uncle wrote.

"Bravo," I repeated.

I could almost imagine the look on my father's face, a broad smile that showed how proud he too was of himself.

. . .

A few weeks later, a letter arrived at the house in Bel Air announcing that we had an appointment at the American consulate in a few days.

At the center of so many families' lives, the focus of so many thoughts and prayers, le consul, in the flesh, was just a very tanned, nearly bronzed white man with what seemed like bottle green eyes. Was he the consul himself or just one of the many employees that formed the pastiche of that identity? I didn't know then and don't know now. However, the man we appeared before that day was wearing a thin white shirt with no undershirt. His fingernails were brownish red, with what looked like terra-cotta underneath.

As I sat with my brother and uncle, separated from the green-eyed man by a polished wooden desk, he looked through our papers, a thick file accumulated over the last five years, the blood tests to prove my father's paternity, the TB diagnosis and treatments, even the X-rays of our lungs, both before and after treatment, and later I would learn, character references from my parents' friends, employers and pastor, my parents' pay stubs, bank statements, tax returns, a summary version of who they had to be in order to be allowed to live in the same country as all their children.

"Ta maman, ton papa te manquent?" Do you miss your mother and father? The man leaned across the desk to ask me, then my brother.

Hanging on the wall behind him was a large American flag, the stars literally bursting from the corner square, their spiky edges merging into the wall. Sensing that it was the right thing to do, we both nodded, as if bowing to the flag that our grandfather had once fought against, that our mother and father had now embraced for nearly ten years, that we were about to make our own. As my head bobbed up and down, I felt my old life quickly slipping away. I was surrendering myself, not just to a country and a flag, but to a family I'd never really been part of.

"I'm going to make you very happy." The man picked up a stamp and dangled it in the air in front of us before lowering it on the top sheet in each of our files.

"You're both approved," he said in what must have been official singsong. "You're now free to be with your parents. For better or for worse."

Pour le meilleur et pour le pire, he'd said. Why? I wondered if he knew something we didn't. Besides, what could be worse than waiting most of our lives to spend five minutes with a person who would say something like that?

That evening, we returned to the call center to share the news with my parents.

My uncle furiously scribbled things down, detailing tasks that needed to be performed before we could leave.

"We have to buy the plane tickets," I said, deciphering his words.

"Tell your uncle to buy them. I'll send him the money." My father spoke louder than he needed to, his voice energetic, animated.

"Are you happy?" my father asked me toward the end of the conversation.

I pretended not to hear.

"Here's Bob," I said.

My brother too came to life on the phone with my parents. The three of them were already chatting like old friends, plotting all the things they were going to do.

"Edwidge has promised a bunch of gifts, something for everyone," he tattled.

I reached over and pinched him on the back of the hand that was holding the phone. My uncle slapped my hand away, all the while shooting me a reprimanding glare. Even though we had been expecting it, how could I tell him that I didn't want to leave him? What difference could it make? For better or for worse, I had to go. These were my parents, my real parents, and they wanted me to come and live with them.

Later that week, Tante Denise took me to a pricey shop on Grand Rue to buy me a new dress. I picked one I thought rather fancy. It was bright yellow with a satin camisole and a flounced skirt. Bob's light blue suit was made by my uncle's tailor, whom he'd engaged since he'd stopped taking work to Monsieur Pradel.

On our departure day, we were overfed before being taken to the airport. Tante Denise cooked a large pot of cornmeal and herring and blended beet juice with condensed milk for us to wash it down.

When Nick, sobbing in his cornmeal, asked, "Why do I have to go back to school after my lunch? Why can't I go with them?" Tante Denise wrapped her arms around Bob's and my necks, kissed our cheeks from behind our chairs and ran into her room. Liline's father, Tante Denise's brother Linoir, who'd spent three years working as a cane cutter in the Dominican Republic, had recently come home to die.

That grief compounded by our leaving was too much for her to bear.

Liline, however, was taking things a lot better. She barely knew her father and was terrified of the sunken eyes, dried-up skin, and convulsions through which his illness was manifesting itself. Just as Tante Denise locked her bedroom door, Liline had blocked the door to her heart. She went to see her father only once and swore she would never see him again. And as Bob and I left the house, even though I'd left my treasured copy of *Madeleine* tucked under her pillow, which I knew she had seen that morning while making her bed, she simply told us "Na wè," See you later, while never looking up from her plate.

At the airport, Bob and I tried to keep up with my uncle as he hurried to one of the long lines winding their way to the counters. My uncle was holding our single small suitcase in one hand and a mustard-colored envelope filled with our papers in the other.

Waiting on the line, my uncle began sweating and kept wiping his face until his blue monogrammed handkerchief was soaked. Was he sad? Angry? Nervous? For himself? For us?

Over the years, in my travels, I have spoken to three middle-aged Haitian flight attendants who claimed they were the ones who met my brother and me at the airline counter, took our hands and led us away from my uncle, guiding us to our seats on the airplane.

"You didn't cry at all," one of them said. "You both simply gave your uncle a kiss on the cheek and walked away."

"You didn't make any noise about it," another one said, "but the front of your dress was wet from your tears."

"You both refused to move. Your uncle had to order you to come with me and he got really mad and yelled," the last one said, not knowing that by then my uncle could not yell.

Their faulty recollections have wiped out whatever certainty I've had, if ever, about that day. At different stages my brother and I were probably all of those children—the ones who didn't cry, the ones who quietly sobbed and the ones who refused to leave.

Over the years, I have also met other passengers who believed they saw my brother and me, him in his pale blue suit, me in my lemon-colored dress, tightly gripping each other's hands and pushing our heads back into the seats as the plane took off.

I only remember wishing as we soared into the clouds that my uncle had cried a torrent of tears, had thrown himself on the ground and made a scene, all the while forbidding us to go. He should have blurted out, in his old voice, the sudden revelation that I was really his daughter and that he couldn't live without me.

Sitting in a middle seat next to my brother, who had insisted on the window I had really wanted, I had looked out at the white clouds only once when suddenly it occurred to me that since my uncle couldn't speak on the phone and probably wouldn't write letters to us children, we would likely never be in touch again.

This realization was distressing enough to make me want to close my eyes forever. I encouraged my brother to do the same. In the process we fell asleep, waking up only when one of the flight attendants nudged us to rouse for supper.

By then it was too dark out to see the clouds again. Bob marveled at the fact that it didn't seem as though we were moving. Though we'd eaten what was probably the biggest lunch of our lives, we still cleaned up our tray of plane food, relishing the novelty of the tiny plastic plates on which the Haitian-style rice and beans and American-style grilled chicken breasts were served. After having spread one of his small butter squares on his roll, Bob placed the other one in his pocket, where it melted before landing.

.

We heard our parents before we saw them. Walking on either side of the stewardess who'd taken us from my uncle at the airport in Port-au-Prince, my brother and I made out our names above the din of the people lunging forward, flashing pictures, waving flowers and stuffed animals in the arrival lounge. Our parents' voices, my father's firm and resolute, my mother's brassy and booming, were coming from behind us.

The stewardess loosened her grip on our hands but didn't completely let go as we turned around to find them.

"Are these your parents?" she asked as they approached, my mother sweeping the crowd aside and my father follow-ing more leisurely behind her, apologizing to the shoving victims in her wake.

When she reached us, my mother grabbed us both and pressed us against her chest. I inhaled deeply, taking in her mixed scent of coconut hair pomade and baby powder that formed uneven white lines all around her neck.

My father took care of the logistics, signing a form that the stewardess had until then kept folded in her pocket.

"Bonne chance. Good luck," she said before walking away.

My father bent down for us to kiss him. His beard, thicker and bristlier now, prickled my lips and nose. Still, I followed my brother's lead and wrapped my arms around his neck as I kissed him.

"Where are Kelly and Karl?" asked my brother, already displaying the male sibling solidarity I would later come to suspect all my brothers of. A friend from their building was looking after the boys, my mother said. We'd see them when we got home.

In the airport parking lot, I shivered. Even though it was spring—a concept I'd have to grow accustomed to now, the actual manifestation of seasons—there was a biting chill in the air. Later I'd learn that my father had lost a job that day. He'd asked his boss at the New Jersey handbag factory where he was working if he could leave early to pick us up and the boss had said no. My father had left anyway and on his way out was told he was fired. During the drive to the airport, he decided he would never work for anybody again.

While loading our suitcase into the back of an old beaten-up gray station wagon, my father asked, "How's Uncle?"

"Uncle seemed sad," Bob answered for me. "I think he was sad to see us leave."

"I suppose that's how it is sometimes," my father said in a whisper of a voice. "One papa happy, one papa sad."

Gypsy

Our new home was a two-bedroom apartment on the sixth floor of a six-story brick building in a cul-de-sac off Flatbush Avenue called Westbury Court. Beneath the building ran a subway station through which rattled the D, M and Q trains at all hours, day and night.

At first sight, my parents' living room seemed lavish and plush with its beige wall-to-wall carpeting, its velour-upholstered sofas and chairs, covered in plastic for their protection, and the diagonal mirror cutouts framing a giant velvet print of the Last Supper. I mistook their fire escape, which extended from my parents' bedroom window to the living room's, for an outdoor terrace and immediately began to imagine all of us spending summer evenings out there, looking over the neighborhood while sipping American colas and telling each other stories.

"Don't, and I mean *don't*, ever go out there!" was the first thing my father said to Bob and me after he'd shown us the living room. "Kelly and Karl already know this. It's where the firemen come if there's a fire and they need to save your lives."

He was speaking as though he was already saving our lives by giving us that most helpful order. I pressed my fingers against the accordion bars on the windows, watching my dreams of spending evenings floating above Brooklyn evaporate.

My brothers, whom my mother had gone and picked up at her friend's down the hall, bounced into the room, eager to see us. They were, of course, bigger: Kelly a gangling seven-year-old and Karl a much stouter five.

Karl immediately ran up to me, nearly knocking me off my feet as he wrapped his arms around my hips and squeezed as hard as he could. Looking up, with a broad, crooked smile, he asked, "Are you really my sister?"

I wasn't used to hugs. It wasn't really part of my daily interactions even with the people I loved most, but I let my hands fall on his shoulders and stroked his back. Looking down at him, I wondered if my mother had told him about the time we'd first met, he a baby in my arms. Or did he instinctively know that we were supposed to love one another?

My parents were looking on, both with big grins on their contented faces. They were perhaps moved, amused, pleased that Karl had what could only be called a deep sense of thoughtfulness. Over the years, I would grow used to it. I'd even count on it. He was often the first to offer a chair to someone who was standing, start a conversation with someone who seemed shy. He was the person to call immediately when something terrible happened. But back then his attempt at a hug felt like more. It was, and still remains, the best welcome I'd ever had in my life. It felt like love.

"Of course, she's your sister," my mother answered when I didn't. Her hand pressed against Kelly's back, she was nudging him forward, toward us, but he stood in place, watching Bob. My father's arm was resting on Bob's shoulder and he too was trying to move him toward Kelly.

"Why don't you show your brother one of your toys," my father told Kelly. Kelly's face brightened. He motioned for Bob to follow him. Bob looked up at my father for confirmation, then slowly marched behind Kelly, disappearing down the narrow hallway that led to the bedrooms.

They were barely gone a minute when my mother called them back.

"Vini, come, food." She motioned for us all to move to the kitchen, where the stovetop was crowded with pots and pans. In a corner across from the refrigerator was a small table and four chairs. Since she and my father and the boys had already eaten, she filled two plates with food and put them down in front of Bob and me. Karl was still holding on, slipping onto my lap as I ate my rice and beans, stewed chicken, fried plantains and meatballs.

"I helped cook that," my father said proudly. "It's your welcome repas."

Kelly was watching us with his chin pressed down on the table. Bob ate quickly and asked for more. I wanted to kick him under the table. "They'll think you haven't eaten since they left you," I hissed.

"Let the boy eat," my father said and laughed. He was leaning against the wall, watching as my mother ladled more food onto Bob's plate. It wasn't so much that Bob was hungry, I knew. He wanted to please them. He frankly wanted them to be happy and feeding him was making them happy.

I stuffed my mouth, but didn't swallow right away. I didn't want them to ask me any questions. I didn't want to have to answer anything.

Once we were done eating, Bob ran all over the apartment, with Kelly showing him where everything was. Eventually Karl slipped away and joined them. My father followed. My mother showed me where we were sleeping, in the second bedroom, the one overlooking the train tracks. Aside from the wall with a line of ribbon windows, every other wall had a bed pressed against it. I had inherited a full-size bed from my mother's sister, Tante Grace, who had been living with my parents before we came. Kelly and Karl shared a metal bunk bed with Kelly sleeping on top and Karl at the bottom. Bob's bed was a twin-sized cot, but had the advantage of being closest to the twelve-inch television set that stood on top of a wooden dresser.

"Do you want to go to sleep?" my mother asked.

I nodded, adding "wi." Yes.

She had already placed a flannel nightgown on the bed for me. When I went to the bathroom to brush my teeth, my brothers were there.

"I'm so glad you guys speak Creole," Bob was saying to them. They were already a trio, a team.

My bed smelled of citronella and vetiver, of getting

dressed and going out, rather than of falling asleep. (The scent, I would later learn, was of a brand of fabric softener.) Liline was probably sleeping on my mattress that night, I thought, taking a break from her own smelly one. How could this vetiver-and-citronella-scented bed, I wondered, ever really be mine?

My parents turned off the lights and left the four of us in the dark. A few minutes later, I heard their muffled laughter coming from the next room, as well as the occasional sound of our names. They were already telling each other stories about us.

"Do you see how much Bob can eat?" asked my mother.

"Did you see how Karl wouldn't let Edwidge go?" asked my father.

"I don't think Kelly's quite sure what's going on."

Somewhere below us, the train would clatter by, drowning their voices, and then there would be only silence again.

In the dark, Kelly, whose Creole was a bit halting but clear, whispered, "Are you guys adopted?"

"No," answered Bob.

"They say you two are older than me," he continued, "but it's not true. I'm the oldest."

Kelly's words reminded me of a puzzling, until now, story that Granmè Melina used to tell about a young mischievous billy goat who came across an old decrepit and hairless horse on a narrow trail one day.

Blocking the ancient horse's path, the youthful goat said, "You should let me go first, because I'm older than you."

"You should let me go first," replied the old horse, "because I'm truly older."

"Can't you see I have a beard and you don't?" replied the bouncy goat, laughing. "Aren't beards a sign of old age?"

Kelly's time with our parents was his beard. Indeed, he had spent much more time with them than Bob and I had combined. How much had he and Karl been prepared? I wondered. Had my parents ever spoken to them about us? Had they even told them we were coming until today?

Later they would both tell me that it was as though we'd dropped out of the sky. They had no memories of their trip to Haiti and my parents had told them nothing. (A fear perhaps, as in the letters, of shattering all the hearts involved.)

"I'll tell you a secret," Bob whispered back to Kelly in the dark. "We're really spies from space. We have spy stuff inserted in our heads."

I was continually amazed by Bob's pool of knowledge. Where had he learned this? From comic books that only he and Nick had read? Tales that only the two of them had told each other?

The next morning, before our parents woke up, Karl got out of his bed and crawled into mine. His fire-engine-covered pajamas also smelled like citronella and vetiver. I was beginning to think that all of America would.

Karl was kneeling and had to press his hands against the wall to keep his balance as he leaned down to kiss my forehead.

"It must hurt where you have the spy stuff in your head," he said, raising himself up again.

"It does," I said, feeling myself on the verge of tears.

Soon after he got up, Kelly climbed up on the kitchen counter and found a butter knife, which he carried back to the room.

"I can get the spy stuff out for you guys," he said, smirking as though to prove that he was not only the oldest but the smartest.

"You can't do it," Bob said, closing his eyes to slowly massage the sides of his face. "No one can. What I can do to make us really brothers and sisters is to ask my friends from space to put one in your heads too while you're sleeping tonight. Then we can talk more easily with each other without even speaking. Do you agree?"

Kelly lowered the butter knife and pursed his lips. Karl looked up at my head as if searching for some clue, some sign of disfiguration, which he might also have to carry for the rest of his life.

"Okay then," Kelly said.

"Okay," echoed Karl.

From that day on, we considered ourselves full brothers and sister.

I still marvel now how Bob, then only ten years old, thought of all this, but as strange as it seems, it truly gelled us, started us on our way to becoming a family.

That morning, while our new blood and spy brothers were introducing us to Saturday-morning cartoons, my father, still in his pajamas, carried in what looked like a large black handbag with a small silver latch and laid it carefully on my bed. And though his face was crumpled and there was sleep in his eyes, he seemed eager for me to open it.

Grabbing the latch, I forced it apart, nearly smashing it. My brothers turned their eyes away from the television to watch me run my fingers over my welcome gift.

It was a typewriter, a Smith-Corona Corsair portable manual. Once more, tears gathered in my eyes before I even had time to think of something to say. I remembered asking my father in one of my letters to send me a typewriter. The tellers at my uncle's bank had them. The clerks at the Education Ministry had them. I'd asked my father for one because I thought my uncle should have one too. Not only for his school and church work, but to write back to my father.

Looking down at the perfect beige keys, lined up like big ivory teeth, I couldn't help but feel that I'd received the typewriter too late. What would I do with a typewriter all to myself?

Then in a flash it occurred to me that I could write to my uncle, hundreds and hundreds of letters to impress him with my new skills, my new knowledge, my new life.

"This will help you measure your words," my father said, tapping the keys with his fingers for emphasis, "to line them up neatly."

He meant this literally. He and I both had slightly crooked cursive handwriting. Unlike him, however, I would often line up my pens against a ruler to keep a straight line. Still, they feel like such prescient gifts now, this typewriter and his desire, very early on, to see me properly assemble my words.

In the end, after becoming better acquainted with the machine, I pecked out only one letter to Uncle Joseph. It was brief, telling him that Bob and I were all right, were getting along fine with our parents and brothers and were thinking of him and Tante Denise, Nick and Liline, Tante Zi and

Tante Tina, Marie Micheline and Ruth, and everyone else. My letter was really a list of names, an inventory of the people whose faces popped into my head every day and whose voices echoed in my ear every night.

My uncle did not write back, perhaps wanting to allow us some distance, some time to merge into our family without any meddling from him. He had written to my father, however, sending him a note whenever a friend traveled from Haiti to New York. After reading his notes, my father would always tell us that my uncle had told him to say hello to "Edwidge, Bob, Kelly and Karl." Were Bob and I no longer special to him? I wondered. No longer worth setting apart?

There's a Haitian saying, "Pitit moun se lave yon bò, kite yon bò." When you bathe other people's children, it says, you should wash one side and leave the other side dirty. I suppose this saying cautions those who care for other people's children not to give over their whole hearts, because they will never get a whole heart back. I wonder if after we left for New York, my uncle felt that way.

A few years ago, I discovered, then lost again, a few lines I had typed, in red ink, a couple of summers after we arrived in New York.

My father's cab is named for wanderers, drifters, nomads. It's called a gypsy cab.

Unlike a yellow cab, a gypsy has no medallions or affiliations. It belongs entirely to the driver, who roams the streets all day looking for fares.

Every Saturday morning after we arrived, my father left home extra early, at four or five a.m., to roam for fares.

"Be careful," my mother called out after him with sleep in her voice.

Stirred awake by the shuffle of both their feet, my brothers and I also wanted to call out, "Be careful," but we didn't, because it would have worried my father to think that we too were fretting about him.

After my father left the apartment, my mother would rush back to her room to open the window over the fire escape and watch him start his motor and pull away. My brothers and I would have liked to do this too, but our window did not face the street, and it would have troubled our mother to know that we were also worried about our father.

Once, while working very early on a Saturday morning, my father cut in front of some teenagers in a stolen van and they shot three bullets at his car. He had a passenger dozing off in the back and miraculously neither he nor the passenger was hurt.

He never told us these types of things directly. Instead he recounted what my brothers and I called his street adventures at the Monday-night prayer meetings, where families took turns gathering at one another's houses each week.

"Even my family hasn't heard this," he would begin. "I didn't want to worry them."

Another Saturday morning, three men held a gun to his head and forced him to drive to the Brooklyn Navy Yard, where they asked him to give them all the money he had in the car. When they found out he had only a few dollars in his pocket, they hit his face with a crowbar and ran away. His face was bruised, black and blue and swollen, but given the circumstances, he made out okay, which is exactly what he told the prayer group the following Monday. "I was only in the emergency room a few hours, most of the time waiting for a doctor to see me. Given the circumstances, I made out okay."

Once in a while, throughout my teens, I'd find myself riding in the front seat as my father picked up fares. Often he was taking me somewhere, but picked up the fare anyway.

One afternoon, an old man called my father a stupid idiot because my father had mistaken one street for another. Another time my father picked up a woman who, when he asked her to repeat her address, shouted at the top of her voice, "No one who drives a cab speaks English anymore!"

My father rarely talked back. "What would be the use?" he would say. "I need their money more than they need my service."

Every now and then a passenger would arrive at his or her destination, open the door and run into a building without paying. Others would say they were going to get money and never come back. My father never went after them. His crowbar and gunshot encounters had taught him that something much worse than getting stiffed might be lying in wait.

Yet another Saturday morning, when I was fourteen, as my father was driving me to an extra tutorial at school, I began to ask myself what type of work I wanted to do. Would I be a doctor, lawyer or engineer, as most Haitian adults, including my parents, hoped their children would be? Or would I do something else?

"Do you ever wish you could do something other than drive your cab?" I asked my father.

"Sure," he answered.

I thought I saw his hands shaking, his lips quivering. He bit down on the lower one, hard, to make the trembling stop. He probably thought I was judging him, telling him that what he was doing was not honorable, prestigious, intelligent enough. However, having started, I couldn't stop.

"What would you do if you weren't driving a cab?" I asked, watching his grip tighten on the wheel.

He stared ahead at the busy street as though it were a screen onto which he could project his life. Had his parents wished him to be a doctor, lawyer or engineer? A farmer? A fighter? Had he nursed some other dream for himself?

"If I could do something else," my father finally said, "I'd be either a grocer or an undertaker. Because we all must eat and we all must die."

PART TWO

FOR ADVERSITY

A friend loves at all times,
and a brother is born for adversity.

PROVERBS 17:17

Brother, I Can Speak

In the summer of 1983, when I was fourteen and Bob was twelve years old, Uncle Joseph came to New York for a medical checkup. Knowing that we couldn't wait to see him, my father took Bob and me to the airport to meet him. My mother had insisted that we wear our crisply ironed new clothes, a bright orange sundress for me and a pair of dress pants and an immaculate white T-shirt for Bob. It seemed to me that my parents wanted my uncle to see us at our best, perhaps even to show him that they were taking good care of us, that they'd washed the proverbial part of us that he and Tante Denise might have left dirty. As we stood in the waiting area, I shifted my weight nervously, all the while wondering whether my uncle wanted to see us as much as we wanted to see him.

Emerging from Customs and Immigration, Uncle Joseph looked slightly different than I remembered. He'd gained some weight, and his rounded belly made him appear shorter. Bob and I both ran to him and wrapped our arms around his body. I was nearly as tall as he was now and it felt odd to reach his shoulder, to look him so easily in his eye. He tapped our faces and smiled, then pointing to our father, who was standing a few feet away, walked over to say hello.

My father wrapped his arms around my uncle's shoulders, embracing him, then he took a few steps back to formally shake his hand. Grabbing Uncle Joseph's suitcase, Papa commented that it was heavy.

"I'll let Bob take care of it," my father said. "He's nearly a man now."

My uncle nodded and put his hands together, confirming that it was a good idea. The suitcase had a long strap and our father handed it to Bob, who, gawky but strong, pulled it forward easily. As Bob managed the bag, I found myself walking between Uncle Joseph and my father, with both their arms around me as if it were the most normal thing in the world.

"How's Denise?" my father asked.

My uncle mouthed, "On ti jan malad."

I was amazed that I could still read his lips more easily than my father could.

"What did he say?" asked my father.

"Tante Denise is a bit sick," I said.

"She functions," my uncle mouthed, "but struggles with the diabetes. And now her blood pressure is high too. Like mine."

"Why don't you bring her to see a doctor here?" my father asked.

"Li pa vle," my uncle said.

"She doesn't want to," I said to my father.

"She relies heavily on her herbs," my uncle said. "Her country medicine."

It was a humid afternoon. When we reached my father's cab, Bob, sweating, stopped and waited for Papa to open the trunk. I stepped aside, joining Bob by the car. My father paused and looked into my uncle's eyes.

"Do you see your children?" my father blurted out as though he'd been waiting a long time to say it. "Do you see how much they've grown?"

My father decided it was best that I take my uncle to his appointment at Kings County Hospital the next day. Unlike anyone else, I could now doubly interpret my uncle, both from silence to voice and Creole to English. Sitting next to him in the packed waiting room of the ear, nose and throat clinic, with the glossy posters of decaying necks and lungs looming over us, I saw his cancer come to life in the men and women around us. Some, like him, had had radical laryngectomies and couldn't speak at all. Others had had partial laryngectomies and spoke in breathless whispers by pressing fingertips against various points along the neck. Leaning forward to listen, my uncle seemed to envy those in the latter category their ability to make some of their basic wishes known, even though they could no longer carry on long conversations.

After examining my uncle, the doctor, a young blond man with a cherubic round face and a bowl-shaped mop of hair, pulled out a sausage-sized machine and placed it in my uncle's hand.

"Tell him," said the doctor, "that this is a voice box, an artificial larynx, something that can amplify his whispers and allow people to hear and understand him."

The doctor placed his hand on my uncle's fingers and helped him form a fist around the machine, then he guided it to a spot above my uncle's gullet and told him to speak.

"Speak?" my uncle asked.

The machine buzzed, letting out a clamor of static. The doctor moved my uncle's hand a few inches, then said again, "Speak."

Uncle Joseph opened his mouth and tried to utter a few words, but no sound came out.

The doctor moved his hand a few more inches, then asked, "What did you have for breakfast this morning?"

"Ze," he said. Eggs.

The sound of the word emerging out of his own body in a robotic monotone seemed to shock my uncle, who raised his eyebrows in surprise.

"Keep talking," the doctor said. "What would you like to have for dinner?"

"I don't know," Uncle Joseph said, the mechanical voice a bit clearer now.

His face lit up. He smiled, baring nearly all of his false teeth.

"Where can we buy it?" he asked.

The artificial larynx was sold in a medical supplies store near the hospital. After the doctor's visit, we went there and got one.

Later that afternoon, when we returned to my parents' apartment, my mother had not yet come back from her job at the textile factory, but my father was there, sitting on the blue plastic-covered sofa in the living room and sifting through his mail while occasionally glancing at the television set, which Bob, Kelly and Karl were watching from the floor. Uncle Joseph turned off the television, causing the boys to silently protest with grimaces. He walked over and sat down next to my father, signaling for them to also pay attention.

"I was worried," my father said. "I thought they'd kept you in the hospital."

The plastic squealed under my uncle as he leaned even closer to my father. Reaching into his pocket, he pulled out the voice box and raised it to his neck. The machine screeched with static when he turned it on. Uncle Joseph adjusted the volume, then pressed it more deeply at the curve between his chin and neck.

"Mira, I can speak," my uncle said, drawing out each mechanized word.

The boys rushed over to the sofa, circling my uncle. My father pushed his face closer to my uncle's. His eyes widened as he looked into my uncle's mouth, dumbfounded.

"How's it happening?" he asked.

"It must be a miracle," my uncle said. "What else can it be?"

"Science?" my father absentmindedly offered.

"Science is God's way of shielding miracles," Uncle Joseph replied.

My father took my uncle's hand and led him to a lamp in a corner of the room, so he could better see the machine and its interaction with my uncle's neck. This was their first two-sided conversation in many years and they both seemed to want to move it past the technicalities to a point of near normalcy.

"How does it sound to your ear?" my father asked.

"How does it sound to yours?" my uncle countered.

My father paused to think, searching perhaps for the most tactful and encouraging description of what he was hearing.

"It sounds like yon robo," he replied. A robot.

My father was trying to be more exact than heartening. My uncle was not fazed.

"To my ear," my uncle said, "it sounds like two voices, my own voice inside my head and the one you hear. I know that voice is going to sound strange to people." He was smiling now, showing all of his false teeth. "But it's better than not speaking at all."

That summer when my uncle went back to Haiti, he sold his first house, the one Bob and I and everyone else in the family had lived in with him and Tante Denise. The house was beginning to fall apart and, since everyone had left, it felt too large for just Tante Denise and him. He then built a small three-bedroom apartment for Tante Denise and himself in the courtyard behind the school and church. He also got a home telephone on which he used to call us often. Sometimes I'd call him just to say hello, which felt like a miracle unto itself.

At first I'd say, "Can you believe we're talking to each other?" And he'd say, "Can you?" But after a few minutes, as he caught me up on things, his life, Tante Denise, political news from Haiti, his voice seemed no more unusual than mine or anyone else's. He was expanding his work, he said, adding to the school and church in Bel Air a clinic that was run by Marie Micheline.

Marie Micheline had left her job as head nurse at the other neighborhood clinic and was now helping him with his work. They were together more than ever. She was thirty-seven years old but, from the pictures I saw of her, looked no older than she did at twenty-two. She'd had three boys after Ruth, with two men who, as my uncle put it, again had not loved her enough. I often imagined myself all grown up and my father talking about me in the same forgiving way that my uncle talked about Marie Micheline. Perhaps because he had rescued her not once, but twice, he loved her even more deeply, more unconditionally.

After he left for Cuba, Marie Micheline's biological father had never contacted them, prompting Tante Denise to call her their Moses girl. She was *their* baby, but unlike Tante Denise, who thought Marie Micheline was spoiled, Uncle Joseph thought she could do no wrong.

"She needs to realize she's not a girl playing with boys anymore," Tante Denise would say even after Marie Micheline had had four children.

"She attracts bad, just like she did Pressoir," Uncle Joseph would say, "but she's not a bad person."

On February 7, 1986, my uncle's sixty-third birthday, Jean-Claude "Baby Doc" Duvalier fled Haiti for France, leaving a military junta in charge of the country. The junta, which ruled for two years, was led by an ambitious army officer, Lieutenant General Henri Namphy. A new president, Leslie Manigat, was sworn in on February 7, 1988, my uncle's sixty-fifth birthday. Because Baby Doc's departure had taken place on February 7, my uncle's birthday had become the official date for Haitian presidential inaugurations and swearings in.

Four months after he was inaugurated, Leslie Manigat was ousted by Lieutenant General Namphy. Soon, Namphy was himself deposed by a military rival, General Prosper Avril. In April 1989, a group of former Tonton Macoutes and hard-line Duvalier loyalists tried to topple Avril in a failed coup, creating hostilities within the army.

The battle between the opposing military factions came to Bel Air one April afternoon when one group chased the other to Rue Tirremasse and the wrought-iron gate of the church clinic. Marie Micheline was sitting alone, behind her desk, looking through some notes she'd scribbled on the twenty or so patients she'd seen that day. They were all minor cases, for once, mostly cuts and scrapes and two infants with low-grade fevers. She'd not had to send anyone to the public hospital.

She was probably just reaching over to slip the files into a small metal cabinet beside her when she heard one gunshot followed by a volley of bullets. Looking up, she would have seen a whirl of camouflage racing past the open metal gate. At this point, she may have thought of the forty people who according to newspaper reports had died that week, caught in the crossfire of such battles all over Port-au-Prince. She may have thought of Ruth or of her three young sons, Pouchon, Marc and Ronald, who were due back from school at any time. She may have thought of Tante Denise, to whom she was to give an insulin shot in a few minutes. Of Uncle Joseph, whose blood pressure she also monitored daily at the same time.

She got up from her desk and ran to the gate, hoping to close it before one of the soldiers barged in. But what if someone needed her help? And how would she feel if Ruth, Pouchon, Marc or Ronald was shot because the gate was closed and they couldn't come in?

Neighbors saw her standing in the doorway with beads of sweat gathering on her forehead. Then a bullet whizzed by, bouncing off the gate with a spark.

The street was suddenly blurry, a cloud of dust descending in the wake of speeding military pickups. Had she been shot? In the heart? She clutched her chest and fell to the floor. She never regained consciousness.

Because Ron Howell, a New York journalist, happened to be covering the military shoot-out in Bel Air that afternoon, Marie Micheline's death was the subject of a *Newsday* article published on April 17, 1989. Headlined HAITI STILL STRUGGLING TO SHINE, it was printed next to a color photograph of her funeral procession slowly winding through downtown Port-au-Prince.

Marie Micheline, wrote Howell, was in many ways "a reflection of Haiti and its potential, a flicker of light frustrated in its attempt to shine."

When you hear that someone has died whom you've not seen in a long time, it's not too difficult to pretend that it hasn't really happened, that the person is continuing to live just as she has before, in your absence, out of your sight. The day of Marie Micheline's funeral, when I spoke to my uncle on the phone, I experienced the biggest failing of his new voice. Like distance, it masked pain. Still, his pauses were like sobs, the expansion or contraction of his words mechanical traces of sorrow.

That night I told my uncle a story that I'd just remembered myself. Of being eight years old and carrying a note home from school requesting that my parent or guardian come to my class to spank me, because I hadn't finished all my homework. That afternoon when I got home, I'd given Marie Micheline the note, thinking that she'd go a lot easier on me than either my uncle or Tante Denise. However, the next morning when she went to the school, Marie Micheline took Mademoiselle Sanon, my very tall, slim and prim teacher, aside, and under an almond tree in a corner of the bustling recess yard, whispered in her ear for five minutes.

"What did you tell her?" I asked Marie Micheline as she walked me back to class with a broad smile on her face.

I gripped her soft, small hands, unable to imagine them pounding me with the stiff cow leather whip, the rigwaz, with which parents and teachers often thrashed their children's behinds or palms.

"I'm going to take care of her and her entire family at the neighborhood clinic for a year," she said. "They'll never have to wait and they'll never have to pay. For that, she won't send anyone in your class home with spanking letters for a month."

"Just a month?" I asked.

"That's the best I could do," she said.

"Her own children," my uncle said at the end of my story. "How can four children lose their mother in an instant like that?"

Fearful of losing them too, he was going to try and get a

visa for Ruth and the boys to join some of Marie Micheline's biological mother's relatives who were now living in Canada.

Before she was buried, a coroner had determined that Marie Micheline died from a heart attack. But when I spoke to Tante Denise, who cried as though she were hollering to the heavens in protest, she said that no one could convince her of a simpler truth: that watching the bullets fly, the violence of her neighborhood, the rapid unraveling of her country, Marie Micheline had been frightened to death.

The Angel of Death
and Father God

In 1990, General Prosper Avril resigned, making room for the December 1990 elections, in which a young priest named Jean-Bertrand Aristide, who had developed a massive following through his bold sermons against the Duvaliers, won 67 percent of the vote. Aristide was sworn in on February 7, 1991, my uncle's sixty-eighth birthday.

I remember talking to my uncle that night. After accepting my birthday wishes, he moved on to Aristide, saying that in the young priest he saw flickers of his onetime hero, Daniel Fignolé. Aristide's firebrand speeches and his political party, the Lavalas or Flood Party, echoed what Fignolé used to call his woulo kompresè, or steamroller, his throng of rabidly loyal supporters, to which my uncle had belonged.

Like most people, my uncle had voted for Aristide.

"He's certainly the best man," he'd said. "But in my old age, I'm no longer interested in best men. I'm interested in the people around me and what he can do for them."

But only seven months later, on September 30, 1991, Aristide was ousted by a military coup. Aristide fled to Venezuela, then Washington, where he stayed for three years. Still, like most of the population, which had eagerly elected him, Bel Air residents remained steadfast in calling for his return through protests and demonstrations. In retaliation, the army raided and torched houses and killed hundreds of my uncle's neighbors.

My uncle managed to stay out of harm's way by avoiding the demonstrations and all other overtly political activity, including speaking out against the military from the pulpit of his church. Still, every morning he got up to count the many bloody corpses that dotted the street corners and alleys of Bel Air. During the years when he couldn't speak, he had developed a habit of jotting things down, so he kept track of the cadavers in the small notepads he always carried in his jacket pocket. In his notebooks, he wrote the names of the victims, when he knew them, the condition of their bodies and the times they were picked up, either by family members or by the sanitation service, to be transported to the morgue or dumped in mass graves.

Jonas, pt. 20 ans, main droite absente, 11:35 a.m.
Gladys, pt. 35 ans, nue, 3:09 p.m.
Samuel, 75 ans, chany, 5:42 p.m.
Male inconnu, pt. 25 ans, visage mutilée, 9:17 p.m.
Jonas, maybe 20 years old, missing right hand, 11:35 a.m.
Gladys, maybe 35 years old, naked, 3:09 p.m.
Samuel, 75 years old, shoeshine man, 5:42 p.m.
Unknown male, 25 years old, face mutilated, 9:17 p.m.

Over the first weeks of the coup, my father called nearly every day, begging my uncle and Tante Denise to leave Bel Air. They'd go to Léogâne for a few days to visit with Tante Denise's sister, Léone, but would always return in time for Sunday services.

Anxious, my father became angry, shouting at the end of their conversations, "You're responsible. Whatever happens to you there, you're responsible if you don't leave."

I'm not sure why my uncle and Tante Denise never left for good. Maybe it's as simple as not wanting to be driven out of their home.

After Marie Micheline died, I asked my uncle why they, and in turn Marie Micheline, hadn't tried to move to New York like my parents did.

"It's not easy to start over in a new place," he said. "Exile is not for everyone. Someone has to stay behind, to receive the letters and greet family members when they come back."

Plus he had more work to do, more souls to save, more children to teach.

In the fall of 1994, Aristide returned to Haiti, accompanied by twenty thousand U.S. soldiers. Citing the brutality of the military regime and the menace of a mass exodus of Haitian refugees to nearby Florida, then president Bill Clinton launched Operation Uphold Democracy.

The day Aristide returned, Tante Denise suffered a mild stroke. After more than two decades away, my cousin Maxo returned to Bel Air. That fall, I too went back to Haiti for the first time, at twenty-five years old.

On the ride to Bel Air, I looked through the cracked windshield of a hired car and saw more people on the now rutted streets than I ever remembered. On nearly every wall was a mural of a rooster, the symbol of Aristide's Lavalas Party, or of the American military helicopter on which Aristide had flown back to the national palace. There were also monuments to losses everywhere: the charred shantytowns of La Saline and Cité Soleil, the busts and friezes of the murdered: a justice minister, a campaign financier and a beloved priest among thousands of others. Piles of brick and ashes stood where homes and offices had been, places that had been both constructed and destroyed in the time I'd been gone. Chunks of Port-au-Prince, I realized, had been wholly assembled and disassembled in my absence.

In many other ways, however, very little had changed. The crippled beggars were still lined up on the steps of the national cathedral and the used-booksellers' scattered stands across from it. The water women still carried water by the bucket on their heads. The colorfully painted lottery stands were still selling hundreds of tickets to hopeful dreamers. The visa applicants still gathered in droves at the gates of the American consulate.

My uncle's street was now crammed with oddly shaped unfinished concrete homes. The alleys were gutted and filled with trash. Yet, when he showed me his list of casualties, written in handwriting so tiny he had to help me decipher them, all I could see was Jonas, Gladys, Samuel and the hundreds of men and women who'd died, their mutilated bodies eternally rotting under the boiling sun.

. . .

Uncle Joseph and Tante Denise's apartment was painted pink like the old house, except the dining room overlooking the tiny courtyard, which was a bright turquoise. Tante Denise was considerably thinner, her movements measured and slow. Her hair, which she'd begun and then stopped dyeing was bright red at the tips and gray at the roots. She touched it self-consciously when she saw me.

"I don't have my wig." She winced and pushed her head forward even as I moved closer.

She was sitting on a cot in the living room, where she took her naps and sometimes also spent the night. Her swollen legs were propped on a low stool and an open-toed sandal dangled from them. A pedestal fan was spinning in a semi-circle in a corner by the window and occasionally blew a stream of warm air into her face. She was wearing a plain white cotton nightgown, which I was told she wore most of the time. She smelled of castor oil and camphor just as her Granmè Melina had. Her glamour, her elegant dresses, her pretty face, her wigs, her gloves now seemed very far in the past. She, like those buildings, had been disassembled while I was gone. She didn't recognize me at first.

"It's Edwidge," I said, feeling like a stranger now not just to her but to Bel Air and to Haiti itself.

"Mira's daughter, Edwidge?" she said. Her lower lip was drooping, slightly slurring her speech.

Grabbing my hand with more strength than I expected, she pulled me down on her lap as if I were still a child.

"Edwidge, let me tell you a story," she said, pressing her elbows hard into my ribs.

The story she told, slowly, haltingly, with her arms braced tightly around my body, was about God and the Angel of Death. It was one of Granmè Melina's stories, one that Granmè Melina said you told to keep death away. In the end, Granmè Melina stopped telling that story because she had *wanted* to die.

"One day," began Tante Denise. A line of drool trickled from one side of her mouth, which I kept dabbing with a towel that draped the back of her chair.

"Father God and the Angel of Death were strolling together in a neighborhood like Bel Air, in a very crowded city like Port-au-Prince," she continued.

During their walk, the Angel of Death would stop in front of many houses and say, "A man died here last month. I took him." Then as they continued down the street, the Angel of Death added, "I removed a grandmother from this house yesterday."

"I make people and you take them," said Father God. "That's why they like me more than they like you."

"You think so?" asked the Angel of Death.

"I certainly do," said Father God.

"If you're so sure," said the Angel of Death, "why don't we both stop here on Rue Tirremasse and each ask the same woman for a drink of water and see what happens?"

So Father God rapped on the nearest door and when the lady of the house opened it said, "Madame, can I trouble you for some water?"

"Non," the woman answered, irate. "I don't have any water to spare."

"Please," said Father God. "I'm parched."

"Sorry," said the woman, "but I can't spare any water. The public tap has been dry for days and I have to buy water by the bucket from the water woman, who's doubled the price. So I only have enough water for myself and my family."

"I'm sure you'd give me some water if you knew who I was," said Father God.

"I don't care who you are," said the woman. "The only one I'd give my water to right now is the Angel of Death."

"But I'm God," insisted Father God. "Why would you give your water to the Angel of Death and not to me?"

"Because," the woman said, "the Angel of Death doesn't play favorites. He takes us all, lame and stout, young and old, rich and poor, ugly and beautiful. You, however, give some people peace and put some of us in war zones like Bel Air. You give some enough food to stuff themselves, while others starve. You make some powerful and others defenseless. You make some healthy and let some get sick. You give some all the water they need while some of us have very little."

Bowing his head in shame, Father God walked away from the woman, who, when the Angel of Death came to her door, gave him all the water she had in the house.

"And because of this," Tante Denise concluded, unaware, it seemed, of even my body, as heavy and limp now as hers, on her lap, "the Angel of Death did not visit this particular woman again for a very long time."

You're Not a Policeman

Tante Denise died from a massive stroke the day after my uncle's eightieth birthday, in February 2003. She was eighty-one years old. My father and I flew to Haiti together for the funeral.

This was my father's third trip to Haiti in the thirty-two years since he'd first left and my twentieth-fifth in nearly a decade. After that first trip in 1994, I returned often, not always to the capital but also to other parts of the country, to help teach a beachside summer abroad course for American college students. I also traveled with documentary filmmakers, went to interview artists for art catalogs, attended academic conferences and even went back for several weeks to write a short book on carnival in a southern city, Jacmel.

During those trips, when my workload and logistics didn't allow me to make it to Bel Air, my uncle came to see me, in hotel rooms, conference halls, libraries and university classrooms. I felt guilty, however, when I didn't make it to the apartment in Bel Air because it was the only way I would get to see Tante Denise, who no longer ventured outside because she was not steady on her feet.

Whenever I could, though, I would add a few extra days to my trips for a stay in Bel Air. During those visits, my uncle liked for me to attend Sunday services at his church, where he would introduce me to his congregation, which over the years had more or less capped at about seventy-five people, most of them middle-aged or older.

During those Sunday-morning services, I would stand awkwardly in front of this group, filled with faces I barely recognized and who, without my uncle's introduction, would not have known me at all, and I would tell them how happy I was to see them. After I returned to my seat, my uncle would share a bit of my family history, how my father and mother had met, how they'd left me and my brother Bob with him when they'd gone lòt bò dlo, to the other side of the waters.

"We're here for a funeral," my father told the immigration officer who silently examined our American passports at Toussaint Louverture Airport. My father and I had both become naturalized U.S. citizens exactly ten years after we'd received our green cards and we both felt a bit traitorous as the officer hastily scribbled his signature on our foreigners' designated customs forms.

Pushing our luggage cart out into the sunlight, my father seemed to shrink a bit, the way he always did in unfamiliar surroundings. In the parking lot outside the airport, Uncle Joseph walked toward us and grabbed his hand, pumping it a few times before letting go. At eighty, Uncle Joseph looked a lot younger than my father. Unlike Papa, he was neither balding nor graying, and he was robust-looking and muscular as a result of a lifelong habit of walking pretty much everywhere. Soon, my aunt Zi parted a crowd of greeters, screaming my father's name. Tante Zi and Uncle Joseph had the same deep dark skin, the same pronounced, calabash-shaped forehead. Shorter than my father by at least a foot, Tante Zi grabbed him by the shoulder, kissed him all over his face, then tried to lift him off the ground. When she couldn't raise him, she turned my way and, while nearly toppling me over, buried her face in my neck the way she used to when I was a girl.

Reaching into his shirt pocket, my uncle pulled out his voice box and said, as if we were learning this for the first time, "Mira, Edwidge, you heard? Madam mwen mouri." My wife is dead.

During the ride into Bel Air, we were stopped at a road-block by two policemen with Uzis, who scolded the taxi driver for having an outdated driver's license but released him for a bribe of twenty Haitian dollars, which the cab-driver told us, rather forcefully, would have to be added to the fare. My uncle and Tante Zi said they wouldn't pay the bribe, but before the driver could ask us to step out, my father agreed. The ride was already costing us so little, my father said. The policeman probably would not have stopped the driver had he not noticed that he was carrying people from abroad.

I have rarely had these types of encounters outside of Bel Air, outside of Port-au-Prince, I told my father.

Nowhere are these types of things more likely to happen than in Bel Air, Tante Zi echoed.

"My wife just died," Uncle Joseph told the driver when he

dropped us off in front of his church. My uncle wanted the policeman's voluntary consideration, the driver's sympathy. He wanted to believe that his loss could change the way others acted toward him.

"My condolences," replied the driver as he accepted double the fare plus the bribe money.

My father was rarely on the other end of this type of exchange. He was usually the driver, not the one being driven. It occurred to me that perhaps he felt he had to make up with this one man for some of the wrongs that had been done to him at the wheel of his cab.

My father was staying with my uncle in his room, sleeping on a cot near the wide platform bed that my uncle and Tante Denise had often shared. I would sleep in a room off the kitchen, not far from theirs.

Soon after we arrived, my father accompanied my uncle to the cemetery to have the family mausoleum cleaned, to the florist to order the wreaths, to the photocopier to have the funeral programs printed. And of course I followed them both everywhere. My father was just beginning to show signs of shortness of breath, which we took to be an allergic reaction to the dust in Port-au-Prince, panting every now and then as we zigzagged through the sweltering, jam-packed streets. But as each errand brought my uncle closer to his final farewell to his wife, it was he who often stopped to rest. Finding a lamppost on the occasional street corner, he would wrap his arms around it and weep.

·   ·   ·

Tante Denise had died the week before Haiti's national carnival would begin. On the eve of carnival celebrations, her neighborhood, her city, was loud and boisterous, with carnival tunes blaring from nearly every other house but hers. We were still two days from Tante Denise's funeral when, wanting a bit of peace and quiet, my father decided to accompany Tante Zi's son, my cousin Richard, the director of the funeral cooperative in charge of Tante Denise's burial, to another funeral in Grand-Goâve, a small town south of Port-au-Prince. I offered to go with them.

I didn't realize how complicated the Grand-Goâve burial would be until we went to pick up the coffin. After parking the car on a pebbly and hilly street and walking down a damp, slippery alley, then climbing a wobbly ladder up to a second-story workshop, we found the coffin maker putting the last touches on a cedar casket, stapling a piece of white cloth to the inner lining and adding a velvet-draped sponge to serve as a pillow. As soon as the casket was done, Richard climbed down to the ground floor and the coffin maker and his apprentice lowered the cedar coffin down to him, carefully balanced on ropes.

Our next stop was a private morgue on Rue de l'Enterrement—Burial Street—that was used by Richard's cooperative. It was the same morgue where Tante Denise's body was being kept. A few days later I would see her there too, just as I was seeing this naked, white-haired stranger being dressed and powdered before he was placed in his brand-new casket.

As we edged into the busy traffic with the coffin and

its occupant roped to the roof of the car, my father, still shocked, whispered to my cousin, "No hearse?"

He couldn't get one in time, my cousin explained, and for such a long trip. But he assured us that Tante Denise would have one for her journey to the cemetery.

I could imagine what my father was thinking. It was a hot day. Won't the sun spoil the corpse? I, in turn, was worried about the coffin slipping through the ropes and the body falling on the ground and my cousin having to pick it up and put it back and in his haste not removing every speck of dust from the old man, adding to his family's anguish at the viewing. But the old man stayed put through the ninety-minute journey and we arrived in Grand-Goâve without incident.

After he'd dropped the body off at the church, Richard took us to the house of a female colleague for lunch. As they discussed cooperative business under a giant avocado tree in the cactus-fence yard behind her house, I realized that Richard was not just an undertaker but also an aspiring politician, whose work was indirectly connected to President Aristide.

After leaving office in 1996, the former priest had won a second term in 2000, in an election whose results were contested by a coalition of opposition parties. Three years later, in 2003, with international funds still frozen over the outcome of the elections, there were massive demonstrations demanding his resignation. His supporters, a large number of them from Bel Air, also rallied in huge numbers, sometimes resulting in deadly clashes between the two groups. An active member of several anti-Aristide groups, Richard, like most future politicians, was hoping to barter for goodwill with good works. This put him in direct conflict with some of the pro-Aristide gangs in Bel Air, many of whom, Richard casually noted to his colleague, wanted him dead.

There were signs, though, that things might be turning around for him, Richard explained. A few weeks back he was coming home late one night when someone flagged down his car, ordered him to roll down the window and pressed a gun to his temple. He heard the slow clicking of the trigger and quickly identified himself. When he heard Richard's name, his would-be assassin begged his forgiveness saying, "Chief, I'm sorry. I didn't realize it was you. You buried my mother a few months back."

Through the entire funeral service for the old man in Grand-Goâve, with family members crying and wailing around him, Richard, who had told the story of his near assassination in such a calm, even amused voice, sat with my father and me in the last pew and with his head leaning against the wall, he slept. Afterward he drove us back to Bel Air at breakneck speed so he could make it to his house before the gangs had a chance to ambush us in the dark.

.

There was no wake for Tante Denise. Fearing that some of the neighborhood gangs might take advantage of a wake to storm the house, Uncle Joseph sent all his visitors home at eight o'clock and locked his doors.

After everyone left, my father and I stayed up with Léone and Tante Denise's brothers, George and Bosi. They passed around a few pictures of Tante Denise looking stylish in many of the dresses she'd sewn herself over the years. My father, Léone, and Bosi and George looked at these pictures and reminisced late into the night about Tante Denise's love of clothes and her making her own, rather badly sometimes when she was in a hurry.

As I dozed off, their laughter startled me again and again.

"Denise, that old goat," Léone said and laughed. "She was a stubborn one."

The morning of Tante Denise's funeral, I took a few pictures of my father and Uncle Joseph getting dressed in the room that my uncle and Tante Denise had shared. As he pulled a navy suit from their shared mahogany armoire, Uncle Joseph waved my father over.

"First time I'm wearing this suit," he told my father.

My father reached for the suit and, like the tailor he once was, expertly examined the material between his fingertips. It looked like silk but was actually a combination of cotton and Lycra, which my uncle had chosen because it allowed the jacket to stretch without losing its shape.

"The next time I wear it," said my uncle, "will be at my own funeral."

When I look at those pictures now, if not for my father's and uncle's solemn faces, I can almost imagine that my father was simply helping his brother with the knot in his tie. Maybe this was something they'd done when they were younger, help each other dress for joyful and sorrowful occasions. But had they? They'd both worked so hard when they were living in the same country that they'd had little time for camaraderie and leisure. Then they'd spent so many years apart that they'd shared very few moments that many other brothers might take for granted.

. . .

My uncle assigned me the job of carrying to the morgue the exquisite white, pearl-beaded, two-piece suit that Tante Denise had chosen a few weeks back for her burial.

When I got to the morgue, I hesitated before entering the small dressing room. But hadn't I, just two days before, watched the undertakers place a suit on a total stranger on the very same metal table that Tante Denise would now be lying on?

Laid out naked, in a perfectly straight line, her body rigid, her eyes sealed shut, Tante Denise actually looked like she was sleeping. But when my eyes wandered down from the folds on her neck to the larger folds on her belly and farther down to her still dark and thick pubic hair, the illusion was gone. The dresser, a cross-eyed young man who looked like he was barely out of his teens, reached between her thighs and brusquely spread her legs apart. He then lifted her arms, letting them drop with a thump once he'd placed her gloves on them. Her head fell back as he slipped her undershirt over it and I reached for it, quickly placing my hand between Tante Denise's pageboy wig and the metal table.

"Leave it to me, please, miss," the young man said in a voice so deep it sounded like it was coming out of someone else's mouth. Straightening the wig, which had been sliding off one side of Tante Denise's head, he used a thin sponge to apply a thick layer of dark brown foundation to her face, then brushed two lines of rouge against her cheeks. As he traced some maroon coloring over her lips, she finally began to look like her old self. In death, she'd regained a hint of the elegance and glamour of her youth, before the diabetes, before the high blood pressure, before the strokes, the departures and unbearable losses, which, according to my uncle, had troubled her much more than her physical ailments.

Tante Denise's funeral was a success. It was a hot afternoon, yet still the church was packed, filled beyond its capacity to comfortably seat around two hundred people. Because she was the pastor's wife and had for many years, before she became ill, cooked the free meals for the school's lunch program, many people came to pay their respects. Those who couldn't fit inside the church, neighbors, former and current students at the school, lined up on both sides of Rue Tirremasse.

During the service, my uncle got up from his usual seat at the altar and stumbled to the pulpit's microphone.

"She was my friend, my wife, the woman who stood by me both when I could speak and when I was silent," he said.

I remembered how much he had wanted to speak at Granmè Melina's funeral. At least now he could, I thought. But he was unable to say more, and he walked back to his seat with his face in his hands.

After the service, the mourners packed into cars and buses and followed the hearse through the winding streets leading past the old cathedral, toward the cemetery. I was in the car immediately behind the hearse and watched as some people stopped and looked in, nodding and waving their condolences at my uncle and father, who were sitting up front with the driver. Nearing the giant wrought-iron gates of the cemetery, we got out of the cars and, as is the custom, lined up in several rows to walk the last mile to the gravesite.

I was walking next to my father and uncle when three

shots rang out in quick succession. The mourners scattered in a nervous stampede, leaving us in the middle of the suddenly empty street. The flurry of people disappearing around street corners and down alleys seemed hazy and unclear. My heart was beating fast, a pool of sweat gathering on my face. Was this how Marie Micheline felt before she died?

My father's fingernails were digging into my forearm.

"Edwidge!" he called out, alarmed.

"Papa," I said, trying hard to focus on his worried face.

"You look like you're about to faint," he said.

My uncle had drifted away toward a group of church ushers who were trying to gather our mourners together again. The trouble was over, the ushers were calling out. The storm had passed. We could proceed.

Suddenly people began to emerge, from behind parked cars, store galleries, alleys, porches. Our procession was slowly moving again, where only my uncle, my father, the hearse and I had stood.

Later we'd learn that the gunshots had been the result of an attack on a cemetery guard by members of a neighborhood gang. The guard had fired three shots in the air to scare them off. But as we finally headed for the gravesite, I will never forget hearing Léone shout, "Denise, sè mwen, sister, what is this, a twenty-one-gun salute? You're not in the military, Denise. You're not a policeman. Why is there shooting at your funeral?"

Brother, I Leave You
with a Heavy Heart

In late August 2004, Uncle Joseph came to New York for a summer visit. At eighty-one years old, and without Tante Denise to keep him company, he wanted a respite from the increasing number of protests in Bel Air. Uncle Joseph's trip also coincided with my father's first hospitalization since his diagnosis.

I was nearing the end of my first trimester and though I had no morning sickness, I felt fatigued and on some hot Miami mornings found myself weeping uncontrollably when I woke up alone in bed after my husband had left for work. Suddenly being separated from others felt like a much more drastic form of isolation, a sentence of banishment for not being near my dying father. So when Bob called to tell me that Papa was in the hospital, I leaped out of bed and boarded the next plane to New York.

Karl picked me up. (And even that felt odd, for it was my father who always did the picking up from airports.) My mother and Uncle Joseph were in the backseat of Karl's car. I could see that Uncle Joseph had lost a few pounds since Tante Denise's funeral—mostly from eating less, he said, now that his wife was gone—yet he looked sporty and fit. Like my mother's, his face also betrayed a hint of fear, which I immediately recognized: it was about my father.

"So how's the patient?" I asked, trying to ease the obvious gravity of the moment.

"You'll see for yourself," Karl said, his face unreadable in profile. "We're taking you to him now."

Could it have happened so quickly? I wondered. Only a few weeks after my father's diagnosis was I being ushered to his bedside to say good-bye?

"What does the doctor say?" I asked.

"Not much," Karl answered. "He's getting IVs. He's also getting respiratory treatment, but they're not going to keep him there long. The doctor's already told us that."

It astounded me how quickly it was possible to give up on someone as sick as my father. Before my father's illness, I'd thought that the sicker a person was, the harder doctors would try to save him. Not so, it seemed.

When we got to the hospital, I watched my uncle sprint down the long corridor toward my father's room. Although he had high blood pressure and an inflamed prostate, the only obvious signs of his being eighty-one were his bifocals and the way his body tilted slightly toward one side. He was wearing his usual dark suit and tie and carrying an oversized Bible that he kept tucked under his armpit.

Before we entered my father's room, my mother, whose

hands were burdened with a bag filled with food-packed Tupperware, waited for us to be all grouped together. Her eyes filling up with tears, she said, "If you look sad, you'll make him sadder. So please, look hopeful." And then just as though magic dust had been sprinkled into her weary and reddened eyes, her face brightened with a hopeful grin.

My father's bed was next to the window, giving him a clear view of the parking lot below. But his eyes remained fixed on a television set bolted on the opposite wall.

He wasn't expecting me. Lowering his oxygen mask, he wrapped both his arms around me when I leaned over to say hello.

His body was even smaller than the last time I'd seen him, yet his face looked round and full from the prednisone. He also appeared relaxed, calm, as though relishing the brief respite the hospital allowed him from having to cope with his illness on his own. There, at least, he could turn it over to the doctors and nurses to manage for a while.

"How's Fedo?" he asked.

"Good," I said.

"Married life?"

He slid his finger over my blouse, checking to see how much the baby had grown. I was still not showing. I simply looked like I had put on a few pounds.

Turning to my uncle, my father winked. I hadn't had a chance to tell my uncle I was pregnant. His phone in Bel Air wasn't working. I probably should have told him sooner, written him a letter, but as with my parents I hadn't found the right tone or time.

"Your daughter," my father said, teasing my uncle. "And she doesn't even tell you you're going to be a grandfather."

My uncle's hands came together in a joyful clap.

"Denise would have been so glad," he said.

My father was discharged from the hospital the next day. After consulting with Dr. Padman, a resident prescribed around-the-clock oxygen. Once the tanks were delivered, my father stopped working. His daily routine was now centered around a few activities. He would wake up in the morning and walk to the bathroom to shower and brush his teeth. He'd then return to bed, where my mother would bring him a breakfast of tea and soup or sometimes eggs—scrambled or boiled—and bread or cornmeal and herring. Along with his breakfast, he would take his first series of medicines, both herbal and pharmaceutical. Then he would pray out loud as though conducting a boisterous one-sided conversation with God.

His prayers were most often about his illness—"God, if you see it fit to cure me, please do. If not, your will be done"—but he also prayed for me and my brothers, for our safety and well-being. He prayed for patience and strength for my mother, who was caring for him. He asked God to bless her for taking care of him. He prayed for a favorable outcome to the American presidential elections, for peace in Haiti and in the world in general.

The week after my father left the hospital, my uncle would rise early to pray with him. Sleeping in the room next to my father's, I would sometimes be awakened by their combined voices, my father's low, winded, my uncle's loud, mechanical, yet both equally urgent in their supplications.

Sometimes, my father remained quiet while my uncle alone implored. "God, do not forsake your servant now. He's sixty-nine years old. He has so much yet to experience. He'd so like to live to rejoice in all the promises you've made to those who serve you. He'd like to watch his progeny flourish, to see the generations emerge before him. He would glorify your name if you were to grant him your grace and lengthen his days. Were you to allow him to return from where he's standing now on the edge of the valley of death, he'd have a testimony to match that of many of your prophets."

After the morning prayers, my uncle would sit in a folding chair at my father's bedside. To fill the silence, my father would attempt to start a conversation, recalling a person they'd both known or some incident they'd shared.

One morning my father asked, "What became of the Syrian you used to work for?"

Scratching his widow's peak, my uncle replied, "He's now one of the richest men in Haiti."

"What about the Italian I worked for?"

"He went from selling shoes to somehow making them."

Then glancing at me, my father asked my uncle, "Do you remember when you wrote me that letter saying that a boy had beaten Edwidge in school?"

Remembering neither beating nor boy, I asked, "When was that?"

"You must have been six," my uncle said. "In primary school."

"I was so mad," my father said, turning over on his side on the bed, "I wanted to get on a plane right then and there, forget everything and go back home to my children."

"That's when I stopped reporting all their cuts and scrapes," my uncle said.

More, please, I wanted to say. *Please tell me more. Both of you, together, tell me more. About you. About me. About all of us.* But my father began coughing, so my uncle leaned over and whispered, "Ush, Mira. Just rest."

Every day at lunchtime, my father would leave his bed and venture downstairs, where he had a desk in a corner of the dining room. There he'd sit and sort through his mail and, whenever he was able to, return phone calls. My uncle would take advantage of this time to nap or walk around our neighborhood. My father would also make an effort to come down to the living room whenever his friends came by. Later, the trips downstairs, even the trips to the bathroom, would become too difficult, and he'd have no choice but to receive his guests in bed.

At five p.m. every day, my father would slowly make his way back upstairs. Sometimes he'd linger a bit longer to have an early dinner, but most often my mother brought supper to him in his room at around seven. Usually it was something light, steamed vegetables or a simple stew. Sometimes, however, he would get a craving for take-out fried chicken and plantains, and either Bob or Karl would stop at a nearby restaurant and pick them up for him before coming over to the house to help bathe him. After his bath and supper, he'd take his final round of medications for the day and then settle in for an evening of television watching.

Over the years my father had accumulated an extensive collection of Haitian-produced movies and professional wrestling tapes. He would watch his favorites of those over and over until he knew all the dialogue. Whenever I watched with him, whether it was a Haitian movie or wrestling, he'd brief me on the scenario, forgetting that he had done so many times before.

He did the same to my uncle whenever my uncle would sit with him in the evenings. My uncle, who never watched anything on television but a few minutes of the evening news, unsuccessfully feigned interest, but ended up grimacing disapprovingly as my father became lost in the spectacles.

In early September, my uncle began packing. School was starting in Haiti and he had to go back to his students and church.

One night after my father had fallen asleep, my uncle asked to speak to me alone in the guest room where he slept. He was wearing a sleeveless undershirt and as he raised the voice box to his neck, I could see the tracheotomy hole throb with every breath.

"I have a thought concerning your father," he said. "I know a doctor in Haiti. He's the head of the national sanatorium. I think he can help."

Remembering the mountaintop national sanatorium as a place to which people, like Liline's cousin Melina, were often exiled before their deaths, I answered defensively, "Papa doesn't have tuberculosis."

"I know," he replied. "But this doctor has had to deal with all kinds of lung diseases. He can help. I've already discussed it with your father. He can't go now. With the oxygen, it's too much to manage. I'm thinking maybe you can pay for a plane ticket and a hotel for the doctor to come here to examine him."

My father wanted none of it.

"I can't bring that doctor here," my father told me the next day. Though he seemed touched by my uncle's suggestion, he also understood the futility of it. "It would be a waste of time and money."

The morning of my uncle's departure, he stopped several times in the narrow hallway while walking from the guest room to my father's bed. Pressing his face against the wooden panels, he was crying. Before entering my father's room, he pulled a handkerchief from his shirt pocket and wiped his eyes.

That morning, my uncle prayed the longest he had ever prayed at my father's bedside. My father closed his eyes and listened quietly, only occasionally chiming in with "Yes. Thank you."

"Lord," my uncle said, "You already know our deepest wish. You know how much it would please us to see your servant rise from this bed and live and work again among those who are well. You know how even the angels would hear our cries of jubilation if his pain were to disappear. You know how much wisdom he would gain, how much insight he'd have to share with others who take their lives for granted."

My uncle lowered the hand that wasn't holding the voice

box and pressed it against my father's forehead. He then recited the Lord's Prayer, encouraging me to join with a nod of his head.

"So you're going?" my father said when we were done.

Maybe I should have convinced my uncle to stay. Maybe it would have helped, done my father some good, helped them both.

"I must go," my uncle said.

"Okay," my father said, "but don't frighten the others in Haiti. Don't tell them about the hospital and the oxygen. Don't make it sound like I'm on my deathbed."

"I won't," my uncle promised. Then, stroking my father's prednisone-rounded face, my uncle said, "I will keep praying for you."

A hush came over them, just long enough to make me think that if he stayed even a minute longer Uncle Joseph might miss his plane. The silence was broken by the youngest of my uncles, Franck, who lived not too far from my father in Brooklyn, honking his car horn downstairs.

"Brother, I'm going, but I'm leaving you with a heavy heart," Uncle Joseph told my father. "I really am."

Reaching up to shake my uncle's hand, my father said, "I know you are."

"I don't know if or when we'll see each other again," my uncle said.

"God knows," my father said.

Then my uncle slapped his forehead the way he did when he remembered something that had previously slipped his mind.

"I'll be coming to Miami in October to visit some churches," he said. "I'll come up and see you then."

My uncle was aiming for my father's forehead, but fell short, his mouth landing on the bridge of his nose. Still it ended up being a gentle kiss, like a grown man kissing a sick child, partly with love, but mostly out of fear.

"Why don't you walk Uncle out," my father said to me, to avoid, I am certain now, having me see him cry.

I followed Uncle Joseph down the steps and to the door of my uncle Franck's car. That morning the tilt of his body seemed a little more pronounced.

"You know we can't all stay together all the time," he said.

Knowing how much my father would not only miss but worry about him, I stood there on my parents' tree-lined street and waited until the car had turned the corner and was completely out of sight.

·

In mid-October, my husband and I learned our child's gender from our midwife, Colleen, at the Miami maternity center where we'd chosen to have our baby. Based on how quickly my belly had grown in a few weeks, I was sure I was carrying twins, while my husband was convinced it was a boy. So during the sonogram, rather than marvel at the crescent-shaped bubble that was our daughter, my husband was looking for a penis and I for a sibling.

My daughter's sex, however, was not what we discussed most that afternoon. Colleen pointed out that I had a low-lying placenta, which was usually self-correcting but could complicate the delivery if it remained unchanged. Statistically three out of four such cases resolved themselves, she said, and the placenta drifted upward as the pregnancy progressed; however, it was something we'd need to keep an eye on.

"If you're going to have a problem, that's the one you want," Colleen added in a gentle, comforting voice. "It's not a huge deal."

Still I worried, imagining mine being the one out of the four placentas that never budged. I called my parents to tell them.

"Don't worry," my mother said. "The body knows what it's doing."

Even though it seemed that was no longer the case for my father.

"You're just like us," my father added, now ignoring the placenta matter altogether. "Your mother and I had our girl first. You'll have to follow us further with three boys."

"No way," I said. "I think I'm just having this one."

"God didn't make us with one eye," he said. "You don't want to parent an only child."

My father was having a good day. The night before, he'd slept more than six hours and in the morning had experienced fewer coughing spells than usual. I could always tell when he was having a good day because our conversation would slowly drift beyond his health and my pregnancy to broader topics, mostly Haitian news items he'd heard about on the radio or seen on television.

That night we discussed Tropical Storm Jeanne, which had struck Gonaïves, Haiti's fourth-largest city, the week

Uncle Joseph had left New York. Jeanne had displaced more than a quarter of a million people and left five thousand dead.

During his illness, whenever my father would bring up news-related deaths such as the ones from Jeanne, I'd try to steer him away from the subject. Knowing that he was often, if not always, thinking about his own death, I feared that other deaths might further demoralize him.

Still pondering Tropical Storm Jeanne, my father said, "Gonaïves is still underwater. I've seen the pictures. In one of the hospitals, patients drowned in their beds. Children were washed away." His wheezing made him sound like a hasty witness. He'd watched the images so many times that he'd dreamed he was there.

Did these dreams make him grateful to be dying the way he was? Or maybe he envied the others their mutual sinking, their communal vanishing. But isn't death, no matter how or when it takes place, always solitary?

"I've been trying to call Uncle in Haiti this week," he said, "but his phone isn't working."

I too had been trying to reach my uncle with no success. However, it wasn't unusual for his phone to be out of service for weeks, even months.

The last time my father had heard from Uncle Joseph, seven days before, Uncle Joseph had called to give him the telephone number of the doctor who was the head of the sanatorium in Port-au-Prince.

"It can't hurt to speak to him," my father recalled him saying.

"I'm worried," my father added now. "He's called nearly

every other day since he left to ask how I'm doing. All of a sudden seven days go by and I don't hear from him."

"I'm sure he's okay," I said. "Otherwise we would have heard something."

Tropical Storm Jeanne had caused relatively little damage in Bel Air. Instead, another kind of storm was brewing there. After September 30, 2004, thirteen years since President Jean-Bertrand Aristide was removed from power the first time and six months since the second time, the protests became a daily event in Bel Air. They usually started outside the small square in front of Our Lady of Perpetual Help, a bullet-riddled Catholic church down the street from my uncle's apartment and church. After Aristide's second ouster, in February 2004, the UN Security Council had passed Resolution 1542 establishing the Brazil-led MINUSTAH, Mission des Nations Unies pour la Stabilisation en Haiti, a stabilization mission. More than eighty people had died when the Haitian national police, operating in collaboration with MINUSTAH soldiers, had clashed with neighborhood gangs during the demonstrations. Headless bodies, including those of two policemen, had been found in different parts of the capital.

That night, along with the newspaper articles that reported these events, I searched the Internet for images of Bel Air. Above a cloud of smoke rising from a burning tire, I saw the wine-colored gates of my uncle's church. I enlarged and rotated the picture as much as I could, hoping to find the church's plain metal steeple or the narrow staircase that led to the classrooms on the bottom floor. Or the courtyard corridor from which you could look up and see my uncle's wrought-iron-framed dining room window. And not too far from it, the jalousies on the recently added third-story apartment where my cousin Maxo lived with his second wife, Josiane, and his five young children, who had all been born since he'd returned to Haiti in 1995.

The next day, I called my uncle Franck in Brooklyn to see if he'd heard from Uncle Joseph. He had the phone number of one of Uncle Joseph's neighbors, and also a number for one of Tante Denise's cousins, Man Jou, but he tried not to use those numbers to reach him. Given the demonstrations and gang activity and beheading threats, Uncle Franck reminded me, each time Uncle Joseph left his house to return a phone call, or even when he did not leave his house, he was putting his life in danger.

Beating the Darkness

On Sunday, October 24, 2004, nearly two months after he left New York, Uncle Joseph woke up to the clatter of gunfire. There were blasts from pistols, handguns, automatic weapons, whose thundering rounds sounded like rockets. It was the third of such military operations in Bel Air in as many weeks, but never had the firing sounded so close or so loud. Looking over at the windup alarm clock on his bedside table, he must have been startled by the time, for it seemed somewhat lighter outside than it should have been at four thirty on a Sunday morning.

During the odd minutes it took to reposition and reload weapons, you could hear rocks and bottles crashing on nearby roofs. Taking advantage of the brief reprieve, he slipped out of bed and tiptoed over to a peephole under the staircase outside his bedroom. Parked in front of the church gates was an armored personnel carrier, a tank with mounted submachine guns on top. The tank had the familiar circular blue and white insignia of the United Nations peacekeepers and the letters UN painted on its side. Looking over the trash-strewn alleys that framed the building, he must have thought, among other things, that he was glad Tante Denise was dead. She would have never survived the gun blasts that had rattled him out of his sleep. Like Marie Micheline, she too might have been frightened to death.

He heard some muffled voices coming from the living room below, so he grabbed his voice box and tiptoed down the stairs. In the living room, he found Josiane and his grandchildren: Maxime, Nozial, Denise, Gabrielle and the youngest, who was also named Joseph, after him. Léone, who was visiting from Léogâne, was also there, along with her brothers, Bosi and George.

"Ki jan nou ye?" my uncle asked. How's everyone?

"MINUSTAH plis ampil police," a trembling Léone tried to explain.

Like my uncle, Léone had spent her entire life watching the strong arm of authority in action, be it the American marines who'd been occupying the country when she was born or the brutal local army they'd trained and left behind to prop up, then topple, the puppet governments of their choice. And when the governments fell, United Nations soldiers, so-called peacekeepers, would ultimately have to step in, and even at the cost of innocent lives attempt to restore order.

Acting on the orders of the provisional government that had replaced Aristide, about three hundred United Nations soldiers and Haitian riot police had come together in a joint operation to root out the most violent gangs in Bel Air that Sunday morning. Arriving at three thirty a.m., the UN soldiers had stormed the neighborhood, flattening makeshift barricades with bulldozers. They'd knocked down walls on corner buildings that could be used to shield snipers, cleared away piles of torched cars that had been blocking traffic for weeks and picked up some neighborhood men.

"It is a physical sweep of the streets," Daniel Moskaluk, the spokesman for the UN trainers of the Haitian police, would later tell the Associated Press, "so that we can return to normal traffic in this area, or as normal as it can be for these people."

Before my uncle could grasp the full scope of the situation, the shooting began again, with even more force than before. He gathered everyone in the corner of the living room that was farthest from Rue Tirremasse, where most of the heavy fire originated. Crouched next to his grandchildren, he wondered what he would do if they were hit by a stray. How would he get them to a hospital?

An hour passed while they cowered behind the living room couch. There was another lull in the shooting, but the bottle and rock throwing continued. He heard something he hadn't heard in some time: people were pounding on pots and pans and making clanking noises that rang throughout the entire neighborhood. It wasn't the first time he'd heard it, of course. This kind of purposeful rattle was called bat tenèb, or beating the darkness. His neighbors, most of them now dead, had tried to beat the darkness when Fignolé had been toppled so many decades ago. A new generation had tried it again when Aristide had been removed both times. My uncle tried to imagine in each clang an act of protest, a cry for peace, to the Haitian riot police, to the United Nations soldiers, all of whom were supposed to be protecting them. But more often it seemed as if they were attacking them while going after the chimères, or ghosts, as the gang members were commonly called.

The din of clanking metal rose above the racket of roof-denting rocks. Or maybe he only thought so because he was so heartened by the bat tenèb. Maybe he wouldn't die today after all. Maybe none of them would die, because their neighbors were making their presence known, demanding peace from the gangs as well as from the authorities, from all sides.

He got up and cautiously peeked out of one of the living room windows. There were now two UN tanks parked in front of the church. Thinking they'd all be safer in his room, he asked everyone to go with him upstairs.

Maxo had been running around the church compound looking for him. They now found each other in my uncle's room. The lull was long enough to make them both think the gunfight might be over for good. Relieved, my uncle showered and dressed, putting on a suit and tie, just as he had every other Sunday morning for church.

Maxo ventured outside to have a look. A strange calm greeted him at the front gate. The tanks had moved a few feet, each now blocking one of the alleys joining Rue Tirre-masse and the parallel street, Rue Saint Martin. Maxo had thought he might sweep up the rocks and bottle shards and bullet shells that had landed in front of the church, but in the end he decided against it.

Another hour went by with no shooting. A few church members arrived for the regular Sunday-morning service.

"I think we should cancel today," Maxo told his father when they met again at the front gate.

"And what of the people who are here?" asked my uncle. "How can we turn them away? If we don't open, we're showing our lack of faith. We're showing that we don't trust enough in God to protect us."

At nine a.m., they opened the church gates to a dozen or so parishioners. They decided, however, not to use the mikes and loudspeakers that usually projected the service into the street.

A half hour into the service, another series of shots rang out. My uncle stepped off the altar and crouched, along with Maxo and the others, under a row of pews. This time, the shooting lasted about twenty minutes. When he looked up again at the clock, it was ten a.m. Only the sound of sporadic gunfire could be heard at the moment that a dozen or so Haitian riot police officers, the SWAT-like CIMO (Corps d'Intervention et de Maintien de l'Ordre, or Unit for Intervention and Maintaining Order), stormed the church. They were all wearing black, including their helmets and bullet-proof vests, and carried automatic assault rifles as well as sidearms, which many of them aimed at the congregation. Their faces were covered with dark knit masks, through which you could see only their eyes, noses and mouths.

The parishioners quivered in the pews; some sobbed in fear as the CIMO officers surrounded them. The head CIMO lowered his weapon and tried to calm them.

"Why are you all afraid?" he shouted, his mouth looking like it was floating in the middle of his dark face. When he paused for a moment, it maintained a nervous grin.

"If you truly believe in God," he continued, "you shouldn't be afraid."

My uncle couldn't tell whether he was taunting them or comforting them, telling them they were fine or prepping them for execution.

"We're here to help you," the lead officer said, "to protect you against the chimères."

No one moved or spoke.

"Who's in charge here?" asked the officer.

Someone pointed at my uncle.

"Are there chimères here?" the policeman shouted in my uncle's direction.

Gang members inside his church? My uncle didn't want to think there were. But then he looked over at all the unfamiliar faces in the pews, the many men and women who'd run in to seek shelter from the bullets. They might have been chimères, gangsters, bandits, killers, but most likely they were ordinary people trying to stay alive.

"Are you going to answer me?" the lead officer sternly asked my uncle.

"He's a bèbè," shouted one of the women from the church. She was trying to help my uncle. She didn't want them to hurt him. "He can't speak."

Frustrated, the officer signaled for his men to split the congregation into smaller groups.

"Who's this?" they randomly asked, using their machine guns as pointers. "Who's that?"

When no one would answer, the lead officer signaled for his men to move out. As they backed away, my uncle could see another group of officers climbing the outside staircase toward the building's top floors. The next thing he heard was another barrage of automatic fire. This time it was coming from above him, from the roof of the building.

The shooting lasted another half hour. Then an eerie silence followed, the silence of bodies muted by fear, uncoiling themselves from protective poses, gently dusting off their shoulders and backsides, afraid to breathe too loud. Then working together, the riot police and the UN soldiers, who often collaborated on such raids, jogged down the stairs in an organized stampede and disappeared down the street.

After a while my uncle walked to the church's front gate and peered outside. The tanks were moving away. Trailing the sounds of sporadic gunfire, they turned the corner toward Rue Saint Martin, then came back in the other direction. One tank circled Rue Tirremasse until late afternoon. As dusk neared, it too vanished along with the officers at the makeshift command center at Our Lady of Perpetual Help farther down the street.

As soon as the forces left, the screaming began in earnest. People whose bodies had been pierced and torn by bullets were yelling loudly, calling out for help. Others were wailing about their loved ones. Amwe, they shot my son. Help, they hurt my daughter. My father's dying. My baby's dead. My uncle jotted down a few of the words he was hearing in one of the small notepads in his shirt pocket. Again, recording things had become an obsession. One day, I knew, he hoped to gather all his notes together, sit down and write a book.

There were so many screams my uncle didn't know where to turn. Whom should he try to see first? He watched people stumble out of their houses, dusty, bloody people.

"Here's the traitor," one man said while pointing at him. "The bastard who let them up on his roof to kill us."

"You're not going to live here among us anymore," another man said. "You've taken money for our blood."

All week there had been public service announcements on several radio stations asking the people of Bel Air and other volatile areas to call the police if they saw any gangs gathering in their neighborhoods.

It was rumored that a reward of a hundred thousand Haitian dollars—the equivalent of about fifteen thousand American dollars—had been offered for the capture of the neighborhood gang leaders. My uncle's neighbors now incorrectly believed he'd volunteered his roof in order to collect some of that money.

Two sweaty, angry-looking young men were each dragging a blood-soaked cadaver by the arms. They were heading for my uncle.

My uncle stepped back, moving to the safer shadows of the church courtyard. Anne, once a student of his school, followed him in.

"Pastor," she whispered, "my aunt sent me to tell you something."

Anne's aunt Ferna, now thirty-seven years old, the same age Marie Micheline had been when she died, he recalled, had been born in the neighborhood. My uncle had known both Ferna and Anne their entire lives.

"What is it?" asked my uncle.

"Don't talk," said Anne. "People can hear your machine."

My uncle removed his voice box from his neck and motioned for her to continue.

"Pastor," said Anne, "my aunt told me to tell you she heard that fifteen people were killed when they were shooting from your roof and the neighbors are saying that they're going to bring the corpses to you so you can pay for their funerals. If you don't pay, and if you don't pay for the people who are hurt and need to go to the hospital, they say they'll kill you and cut your head off so that you won't even be recognized at your own funeral."

My uncle lowered the volume on his voice box and leaned close to Anne's ears.

"Tell Ferna not to worry," he said. "God is with me."

Because, just as he'd told my father, he would be leaving for Miami in a few days to visit some churches, he had eight hundred dollars with him that he planned to leave behind for the teachers' salaries. So when his neighbors crowded the courtyard telling him of their wounded or dead loved ones, he gave them that money. Because many were bystanders who had been shot just as he might have been shot inside the walls of his house, his church, they understood that it was not his fault. By the time it got dark, however, and Tante Denise's brothers urged him to go back inside so they could lock all the doors and gates, the two corpses had been dragged to the front of the church and laid out. That afternoon, on the radio, the government reported that only two people had died during the operation. Obviously there were many more.

That night after dark everyone gathered in my uncle's room. He and the children crowded together on his bed, while Maxo and his wife, Josiane, Léone and her brothers stretched out on blankets on the floor. To avoid being seen, they remained in the dark, not even lighting a candle.

They could now hear a more familiar type of gunfire, not the super firing power of the Haitian special forces and UN soldiers but a more subdued kind of ammunition coming from the handguns and rifles owned by area gang members. Shots were occasionally fired at the church. Now and then a baiting voice would call out, "Pastor, you're not getting away. We're going to make you pay."

Using a card-funded cell phone with a quickly diminishing number of minutes, Maxo tried several times to call the police and the UN alert hotline, but he could not get through. He wanted to tell them that their operation had doomed them, possibly condemned them to death. He wanted them to send in the cavalry and rescue them, but quickly realized that he and his family were on their own.

At one point they heard footsteps, the loud thump of boots on a narrow ledge above my uncle's bedroom window. Maxo tightened his grip on the handle of a machete he kept under his pillow, just as his father had in his youth. Something heavy was being dragged across the floor above them, possibly the generator on which they relied for most of their electrical power.

It was quiet again. My uncle waited for the children to nod off before discussing strategy with the adults.

"They're mostly angry at me," he said. "They're angry because they think I asked the riot police and the UN to go up on the roof. Everyone who came tonight asked me, 'Why did you let them in?' as though I had a choice."

"Maxo," he said, putting as much command as he could

behind his mechanized voice. "Take your wife and the children and go to Léogâne with your aunt and uncles. If you leave at four in the morning, you'll be on one of the first camions to Léogâne."

"I'm not going to leave you," Maxo said.

"You have to," my uncle insisted. He wanted to paint a painful enough picture that would force Maxo to leave, not just to save himself but the children as well. So he borrowed an image from his boyhood of the fears that a lot of parents, including his, had for their children during the American occupation.

"They're very angry with us right now," he told Maxo. "What if they bayonet the children right in front of us? Would you want to see that? Your children torn from limb to limb right before your eyes?"

Maxo paced the perimeter of the room, walking back and forth, thinking.

"Okay," he said finally. "I'll make sure the children leave safely, then I'll come back for you. You call my cell phone as soon as you can and we'll meet at Tante Zi's house in Delmas."

"You should leave with us," Léone persisted.

I'll never know whether my uncle thought he was too old or too familiar to his neighbors, including the gang members, to be harmed in any way, but somehow he managed to convince everyone to leave. So when the sun rose the next morning, he was all by himself in a bullet-riddled compound.

Hell

Granmè Melina liked to tell a story about a man who one day fell asleep and woke up in a foreign land where he knew no one and no one knew him. Finding himself on his back in the middle of a dirt road filled with strangers, he looked up at the blurry faces around him, which were framed by a gloomy gray sky, and asked, "Where am I?"

"You're where you are," answered a booming voice.

"Where's that?" he asked.

"Where you need to be," replied the voice.

"I didn't ask to be here," the man said, "wherever it is."

"No matter how you ended up here," said the voice, "here you are."

Tired of the roundabout conversation, the man said, "I want you to tell me right now where I am. If you don't, I'm going to be angry."

"Who cares about your anger?" answered the voice. "No one is scared of you here."

Truly upset now, the man said, "Tell me where I am right now!"

"You are in hell," replied the voice.

And since these were long ago times, the man didn't know what hell was, even though he could already see that it was not a happy place.

"What is hell?" he asked.

"Hell," replied the voice, "is whatever you fear most."

The next morning, Monday, at four a.m., Maxo, his children, his aunt and uncles reluctantly left for Léogâne. My uncle sat alone in his room and gathered some papers, including his passport and his Miami plane ticket, which he'd purchased weeks before to visit some Haitian churches there. He was scheduled to leave on Friday, October 29, just as he'd told my father.

The plane ticket bookmarked the Lord's Prayer in his Bible. He would now leave the house, for how long he wasn't sure, but he hadn't wanted to put the children's lives in danger by walking out with them. Besides, he was still hoping that the situation might somehow be resolved. He could talk to the dreads, as the dreadlocked gang leaders were also called, and explain. After all, before they were called dreads or even chimères, they were young men, boys, many of whom had spent their entire lives in the neighborhood. He knew their mothers, fathers, sisters, brothers, uncles and aunts. Some of them had attended his church, his school, had eaten in his lunch program. Many had been to his church for christenings, weddings and funerals. He would often lend them his generator for soccer tournaments and block parties. He had even given many of the U.S. deportees among them jobs as English tutors for his students. The shooting from his roof had destroyed an uneasy equilibrium between him and them, but surely one of them would have a fond memory that could override what they wrongly believed he'd done.

Before heading downstairs, my uncle removed the suit he'd had on since the day before and changed into a maroon pants and gray jacket ensemble he sometimes wore on long trips to the countryside. He put on a pair of old brown leather shoes, which, like all his other shoes, had been repaired and resoled many times. I'm not going anywhere, he wanted his clothes to say. And up to that point he wasn't sure he was.

As soon as he walked down to the courtyard he heard one of his neighbors hissing at the side gate, trying to get his attention. It was barely light, but the streets were already full with vendors hawking their wares and people walking back from Mass, children heading to school and camions and taxis dropping off and picking up fares. His neighbor Darlie, a tall and skinny girl with long braids dangling past her waist, quickly slipped through when he opened the gate and pulled it shut behind her.

"Pastor," she whispered, "last night they took the church's generator and when Gigi tried to stop them, they picked her up and threw her off one of the terraces."

"O bon dye," My God, he mouthed, raising both his hands to his head. How could Gigi, another kind neighbor, have put herself between an armed gang and a generator? And how could he have not heard her screams from his room?

"Is she alive?" he mouthed. He knew better than to use his voice box, which would draw attention.

"One of her legs is broken," the neighbor continued. "She's in the hospital."

My uncle reached into his pocket where he had his passport and plane ticket, and into his jacket pocket where he often kept his Bible, on the off chance there might be a few dollars left. All his money was gone.

"But this is not what I came to say. Pastor, you should leave now. They're coming. Go away quick. They're coming."

She unlatched the gate and slipped out. My uncle was trying to close it behind her when a man's large hand reached in and yanked the metal latch away from his fingers. A short, beefy youth with a small Haitian flag wrapped around his head quickly stepped into the courtyard. He had a face pockmarked with what looked like lines of razor scars. He was followed by another man, this one taller, thinner, with a thin, uneven beard and a white fishnet cap covering an abundant head of long dreadlocked hair. A bald-headed man followed. The last one opened the gate wider to allow in a few others. Then followed another group, then another, all their faces quickly merging into one angry haze. Suddenly he understood the true workings of a mob, one infuriated body morphing into another until they all became limbs to one raging monster.

The courtyard was soon filled with young men. And when he looked up at the balconies and terraces, they were crammed too.

"Pastor," the chief dread shouted, his voice strained and hoarse. "Thanks to you, we lost fifteen guys yesterday and we have six with bullet wounds. Because you let the fuckers in, you need to pay or we'll cut your head off."

The chief dread particularly cited the cases of two young men my uncle knew, both not yet twenty years old. During the raid, a bullet had fractured one's ribs. The other had been shot in the stomach. Their families were afraid to take them to the public hospital, the chief dread said, because, assuming that they were all criminals, the police routinely shot young men with bullet wounds there. They needed money to find a doctor for these men and others, a doctor who would come to them.

The amount he was asked to pay was too impossibly high to even remember. It might as well have been a billion dollars. Hoping to bargain, reason, my uncle reached over and tried to touch the dread's burly arm. The dread shoved his hand aside with enough force to make him nearly lose his balance. As he steadied himself on his feet, my uncle raised his voice box to his neck and said, "Tande."

The chief dread motioned for quiet from the growing crowd.

"I need time," my uncle continued. "I need to make some phone calls. I need to get in touch with my family in New York. I need to ask them to send me some money. My phone is not working. I have to find a phone. Come back this afternoon, at one, and I'll have something for you."

The chief dread looked over at the crowd, then up at the classroom balconies, eyeing those gathered for their approval. He then raised his sizable hands in the air and like Moses parting the Red Sea, signaled for them to scatter. But they didn't go far. Splitting into smaller groups, they stormed the terraced classrooms and began grabbing whatever was within reach: the blackboards, benches. Some detached the doors from the hinges and took off with them. The top dreads moved aside, allowing more people into the courtyard even as they stepped out.

My uncle was completely surrounded, but no one was touching him. Everyone was heading farther into the compound, toward his apartment, the church. From where he was standing, totally frozen in a spot near a small outdoor grill that Maxo's wife sometimes used to cook their meals, he could see many of his neighbors scurrying off with his things: Nana, an old woman limping with a cane, carrying some of his dinner plates, Danielle, a small girl whose mother sold water to him now and then, joining strangers as they walked by with a handful of Maxo's children's clothes. He could now see the navy blue cotton and Lycra suit he'd worn to his wife's funeral, the one in which he wanted to be buried, walking away on some boy's arms. As the crowd rushed back and forth around him—there went the charcoal grill and his windup alarm clock—he did not dare move to the other side of the courtyard, where a plume of smoke was rising outside the church.

They're burning the altar of the church, someone yelled, and some of the direksyon, that is, the school principal's office.

The crowd began heading that way, but he remained in place, not moving. He wanted to go to the church, to see it, to defend it, to reclaim the altar. But what if the crowd decided at that moment to burn him too?

What he couldn't see was the pews and altar being dragged into the middle of the street and set on fire. Part of his office, which was directly beneath the church, was also burned, his papers, including the dozens of notepads in which he'd jotted down words and sentences, his observations about the neighborhood, in good times and bad, they were all scattered now, all over the streets, being trampled, carried away, or burned.

The courtyard was nearly empty now, with everyone's focus shifted to the church. The few people who were still milling about shamefully avoided his eyes as they walked by, one with a handful of new toothbrushes that he'd kept on the night table in his bedroom upstairs.

He had to get out now, finally leave the neighborhood for good. But how would he get through the barricades, where surely the dreads had people waiting, watching for him? As he moved toward the gate, he spotted Anne, the niece of his old friend Ferna, standing there across the alley, watching him. Had she turned against him too? Had her aunt? Anne held out her empty hands, showing that she was carrying nothing. She had not stolen from him.

"Vini," she said. Come.

He went without thinking, letting her drag him by the hand. Walking the slippery incline that separated his house from another small courtyard, he kept his face down, his chin as close as he could to his chest without blocking his tracheotomy hole. He did not dare look back toward the church as a new wave of looters brushed past him, heading there. He might have been tempted to follow them, to try to stop them, reason with them. He thought about all the wounded who might be lying somewhere dying. He thought of their mothers, fathers, standing over them unable to do anything but watch. The country was once again losing a generation of young people, some violent, some bystanders, but all in the line of fire, dying.

The courtyard he and Anne stepped into led to a series of narrow alleyways, some haphazardly paved in slippery concrete, some packed with dirt and mud and others dotted with pools of stagnant dirty water. The neighborhood's labyrinth of corridor-sized alleys was like tunnels, leading everywhere, but alas, only within the neighborhood. He was not too familiar with the path Anne was leading him on now. New houses, shacks, were being built all the time, creating newer and narrower trails. Finally, she opened a corrugated iron gate, pasted together from several rusting pieces, and stepped inside.

The yard was only large enough for a latrine and a concrete water basin capped by a rusting faucet. Without saying a word, Anne's aunt Ferna, a beautifully portly young woman, motioned for him to enter the crowded darkness of her house. Hot and sweaty now, he felt his way past a beaded curtain to a corner between a small dining room table and her bed.

"Pastor, you can stay here until dark," she said. "Then we'll find somewhere for you to go."

The wicker chair she gave him to sit on was much too low and his back ached as he shifted now and then, hoping to find a more comfortable position. But he had to remain there, she insisted. In case someone walked into the house, he could easily slide under the table and remain out of sight. Crouched there, he could hear the normal sounds of the day, a woman chiding her maid for a lunch that had been burned, a father cursing the school master who had sent his son home because the father had not been able to pay that month's tuition. At the same time, some people were walking by saying, "Did you hear, they nearly killed Pastor?"

He heard many variations of this, people dashing to the church to see, to his apartment to find out what they could get. His entire life was now reduced to an odd curiosity, a looting opportunity. He was grateful, however, that no one seemed to know he was there, hiding. Some thought he had actually been killed. Others seemed certain he had fled.

The neighborhood talk soon moved on to other things. Again the more mundane details of daily life. The egg seller came to collect a debt from Ferna. A friend stopped by to braid Anne's hair. The visitors were greeted at the door and not allowed inside. He tried to think of where he might go next. Surely the dreads had now gone to look for him. Perhaps they'd only wanted him to flee, to leave the compound so they could confiscate it. Ferna and Anne had no news. They, like him, had no landline or cell phone. They were even afraid to turn on their radio, afraid that might draw someone's attention. Had they turned on the radio, they might have heard that the Haitian riot police and the MINUSTAH were out on another sweeping operation. This time it was in nearby Fort National, not far from the country's national archives, where twelve young men were shot and killed.

Later that afternoon, my uncle somehow managed to drift off to sleep. Thankfully he had always been able to sleep no matter what. Perhaps it was because he was constantly busy, waking up early and going to bed late. He also liked to walk, often overexerting himself. No matter what, his body could always shut itself down, forcing him to rest.

When he woke up, Ferna was shaking him. He could feel her breath on his face, but could not see her in the dark.

"Pastor," Ferna said, her voice dragging with worry and sleep, "you should go now. You should leave."

"What time is it?" he asked, making sure that his voice box was at the lowest possible volume.

"Three thirty a.m.," she said. Nearly the same time, he remembered, that Maxo, his aunt and uncle and the children had left. Where would he go now? He could go to Léogâne and join them, but would he make it through the barricades and to the bus depot? He could also go to Tante Zi's in Delmas, but would he have the same problem?

He could think of only one solution. Tante Denise had a cousin who lived right on the fringes of the neighborhood, near the perimeters of the gangs' barricades. Her house was somewhere between the Lycée Pétion and Our Lady of Perpetual Help church, where the UN tanks often gathered. If he could make it to her place, then they could wait for an opportune moment when the tanks were there to slip out of the neighborhood.

"You know Man Jou?" he asked Ferna.

She did.

"I'll go to her house," he said. "She has a telephone. I can call Maxo from there. I don't want him to try to come back for me. They might kill him."

Now he could also hear the shuffle of other feet in the dark—Anne's. Anne lit a small kerosene lamp and moved it toward his face.

"You can't go out in your own clothes," Ferna said. "We need to disguise you."

Reaching into an open suitcase laid out by his feet, Ferna pulled out a dark, curly, shoulder-length wig, a wide-rimmed wicker sun hat and a long flowered muumuu large enough to fit over his clothes. He couldn't figure out why she had all these things packed in the suitcase like that. Maybe she was thinking that one day she too might need to escape.

"You must disguise yourself," Ferna insisted again. "It will be light soon and someone might see you."

What choice did he have? He could not let himself be captured. He could not surrender either, to be butchered, to die. So he let Ferna and Anne slip the muumuu over his clothes. As they placed the wig on his head, the hair fell against the side of his face, itching, just as his wife's wigs had when he would kiss her long ago. Though she wore wigs for a long time, he remembered how she often found them intolerable, yanking them off her head as soon as she got home.

Wearing the wig and with the muumuu over his own clothes, he stepped out into the alley with Anne and Ferna at his side. There was an odd stillness to the neighborhood, the houses merging with the murky shadows in the dark. As they guided him up and down the hills and inclines of the winding neighborhood alleyways, he felt like a blind man being led through a labyrinth. Walking briskly, they would occasionally come across a boy stumbling home, drunk. A girl heading to sleep after a night of selling her body. A man, or was it a woman, who, following a furtive look at his very male shoes, quickly hurried past them, head further bent, face further hidden, this person perhaps also a fugitive, perhaps also fleeing.

· · ·

Man Jou bore the balloon-shaped jowls of Tante Denise's clan as they aged. She was often ready with a smile, but even readier with a scowl. She was known for her quick temper, but also for her generosity and sense of humor. So when Uncle Joseph showed up at her door dressed in drag, she opened the door, laughed, then let him in. Her house, like Ferna's, was small, a living room and one even smaller bedroom. However, she had a large bed, with enough room for someone to disappear under it without suffocating.

My uncle spent the next two days at Man Jou's house, sleeping on a twin mattress at the foot of her bed. As he lay there, often after attempting a series of phone calls through which he'd been unable to reach either Maxo and the children or Tante Zi, he would listen to Man Jou's accounts of an increasingly dismal state of affairs. In nearby Rue Saint Martin, the police had ordered four young men to lie facedown on the ground and had shot them at close range in the back of the head. Their bodies were left to rot on the street for more than forty-eight hours, as a gruesome deterrent. In the meantime, the gangs had constructed new barricades near his church with trash and burnt-out cars. Only residents who were on good terms with the gang members were being allowed to enter his street. The gangs had set up residence in his apartment, the school, the church, establishing a base from which to operate on his premises.

"If he ever comes back," the chief dread was said to have declared, "we'll burn him alive."

Limbo

My uncle was able to reach Maxo and Tante Zi on their cell phones the following Wednesday night. They'd exhausted their minutes calling all over town, trying to track him down. Finally they'd refilled their cards and waited for his call.

Once his children were safely settled in Léogâne, Maxo had decided to travel with his father to Miami and planned to meet up with him at Tante Zi's as soon as his father made it out of Bel Air. When my uncle called Tante Zi, whose stationery stand was on Grand Rue, only a few minutes' walk from Man Jou's, Tante Zi decided to go and get her brother.

"Don't come," my uncle pleaded. "Not now, Zi. Not yet."

"We can't just leave you there," Tante Zi said. "You have your ticket. You can leave the country tomorrow. We have to get you out."

The next morning, Thursday, Tante Zi got dressed in one of the all-white outfits she'd been wearing since 1999, when her oldest son, Marius, died of AIDS in Miami at the age of thirty.

At the time of Marius's death, he'd left no trace of his more-than-five-year undocumented stay in Miami. No note for his mother. No bankbooks or jewelry, nothing that could be placed in a sealed pouch and mailed to his family. Because of the void out of which Marius had been shipped to her in a shiny American coffin, Tante Zi always carried pictures of his corpse with her wherever she went and wore only white clothes, as a daily reminder of his passing.

Tante Zi was wearing her mourning garb when she approached the first barricade in Bel Air that morning.

"Son," she called out to one of the many armed young men guarding a narrow path between two shelled-out yellow school buses. One of the men bore an eerie resemblance to Marius, her dark, broom-thin, beautiful boy. She held out a hand to him. He reached back. She quickly pressed a Haitian twenty-dollar bill into it, turning away before the others could see.

"Pray hard," he mumbled. Maybe he thought she was on her way to Our Lady of Perpetual Help to attend early-morning Mass.

He motioned for her to walk past and she did, moving farther into the neighborhood.

This was the first time she'd been in Bel Air since Sunday's operation. She had never seen it so bad. The streets were cluttered with trash. There were empty tear gas canisters, hollowed grenades, spent cartridge and bullet shells and other garbage everywhere. Some houses were missing entire sections from the bulldozing by UN earthmovers.

As she walked through another checkpoint, this one a pile of tires as tall as she was, she raised both her hands over her head even though no one was there. Clutched in her right fist was a white handkerchief, which she waved back and forth to show that she was unarmed. The UN patrols and the gangs' checkpoints were separated by only a few blocks, leaving room for someone like her, who just happened to be on the street at the wrong time, to be shot by both sides.

The sun had risen and a few people were beginning to venture out of their houses. She was trying her best to blend in, walking slowly as though she were just strolling and not going anywhere in particular, but she was also sweating, soaking her cotton blouse and skirt. Not since those long days between hearing the news of Marius's death and waiting for his body to come home had she felt so frightened.

A UN tank was parked a good sprint away, down the hill, near the Lycée Pétion. She and Uncle Joseph had only to make it there before they could consider themselves safe, at least from the gangs. She'd have to find the right trail, perhaps the muddiest, the least-frequented path, through the maze of alleys that would deliver her there.

Filing down the pebbled alley leading to Man Jou's house, Tante Zi alternated between walking too fast, then too slow. Just as she and Man Jou had agreed on the phone, Man Jou was waiting for her out front. They wanted things to seem as normal as possible, just a chance early-morning encounter.

"Would you like to come in?" asked Man Jou.

"Wi, mèsi, but I can't stay," Tante Zi said.

My uncle was sitting on Man Jou's bed, calmly reading his Bible. He was wearing the same clothes he'd had on under the muumuu since Monday. His face appeared hollowed, his high cheekbones—so much like my father's—sticking out a lot more than usual. Looking up and seeing Tante Zi, he seemed relieved but also sad.

"Frè mwen." Brother, Tante Zi said, kissing him on the forehead.

He raised his shoulders and shrugged, which she understood to mean, "Oh, well, things are what they are."

"He doesn't want to do it again," Man Jou said. "He won't wear the disguise."

"Frè mwen," Tante Zi said.

My uncle shook his head no.

"I'll borrow a towel, then," Tante Zi said. "We'll cover his head, at least. If anyone sees us, they'll think he's a sick person, someone we're taking to the hospital."

My uncle was tired of hiding, but most of all he wanted to stop imposing on Man Jou, so he agreed to the towel.

When they stepped out into the early-morning sun, my uncle, even with part of his face covered by the towel, winced from the light. Tante Zi grabbed his hand and pulled him down yet another series of winding corridors and back alleys, their feet splashing in the mud as they went. Though she was yanking hard, dragging him at times, he put up no resistance, catching up as much as he could.

"He was so tired," Tante Zi recalled, "it's as if he had surrendered."

She tried to stay as close to the road that was being patrolled as possible. There would be fewer people down those alleyways and certainly very few gang members. Still, every face seemed menacing. Even the oldest woman peering out from her porch. Even the youngest child jumping rope next to her. Her grip tightened on my uncle's fingers with every step. They had only to make it to the Lycée, to one of the patrolling tanks, she kept reminding herself.

While still in the alleys, they got as close to the road as they could, then Tante Zi dashed across an empty street, still tugging at my uncle. Walking quickly, they followed the footpath by the square in front of Our Lady of Perpetual Help, just in case they had to run inside the church for shelter. Within a few short minutes, they were in front of the Lycée, but the UN patrol was no longer there. Racing past the old cathedral, they merged into the crowd of vendors and slow-moving cars.

That wasn't so hard, Tante Zi remembers reading on my uncle's face. Why hadn't I tried it myself?

"You couldn't have, brother," she said, reassuring him. "They didn't just take your things. They took your legs. They took your heart. You could have walked out of Man Jou's house alone and dropped dead from the shock of seeing the few people who did not want to kill you."

She held him by the elbow as they walked to her stationery stand. She hadn't been able to work every day in the weeks since the demonstrations had started. Catching his breath, my uncle removed the towel from his head. He sat down on a footstool in front of her stand and began wiping the mud off his shoes with a piece of newspaper. Tante Zi offered him water that she was using to clean her own feet and he accepted some. He turned down the food she offered him when they were done. He was suddenly full of plans. He needed to go to the police's anti-gang unit to report what had taken place, to the UN to file a complaint. Maxo was even now traveling from Léogâne and was going to go with him to Miami. My uncle had to stop by a bank to get some money, then a nearby travel agency to confirm that his flight was still leaving, then buy a ticket for Maxo. Were the flights even operating? he wondered. But then again, chaos in Port-au-Prince was often restricted to certain areas only. There could be a war raging in some neighborhoods, while others were as peaceful as . . . usually one might say as a church or perhaps a cemetery, but peace was hard to find now in some churches and cemeteries too.

He also had to stop at a pharmacy for a refill of the medications he was constantly taking for his inflamed prostate and high blood pressure. That same pharmacy had herbal remedies too, tree-bark-soaked tonics mixed with liquid vitamins that, he believed, if not cures, helped the body fight certain illnesses. While there, he picked up a large bottle for my father and another one for himself. These were not very different from the types of hope-laden potions my father's New York herbalist might have prepared, but my uncle, having used such potions all his life, was certain that they would work better simply because they were homegrown.

Once he'd picked up his medication, he took a taxi to the anti-gang unit across from the white-domed presidential palace. During the early Duvalier years, in the late fifties, early sixties, you were not supposed to stop even for a minute in front of the presidential palace or you might be suspected of plotting against the government and risk being shot. Also at that time, if your hair was not closely cropped or if you had something that was beginning to resemble an Afro, you could be arrested. You could also be put in jail for walking around barefoot, like a vagrant, even if you were too poor to buy shoes. These so-called chimères, these young men, some of whom were dying at home from their bullet wounds, and others who were even now crammed into a nine-by-nine-foot holding cell inside the anti-gang building, would not have survived that era either.

Inside the building, the noise was deafening, the cries of complaints from the overcrowded holding cell, the police officers marching in, some of them still wearing balaclavas over their faces even while inside. My uncle quickly walked to a desk manned by one of the special forces officers who was not wearing a mask. Like his masked colleagues, this man was tall and large, larger than most Haitians. Sometimes he'd hear his parishioners say that the CIMO officers were not really Haitian or even human at all. They were machines created by the Americans who trained them to kill and destroy.

"Can I help you?" asked the giant officer at the desk, who looked rather kind and mild, not like a brutal killer at all.

"I'd like to make a report," he said.

His mechanical voice probably echoed throughout the dim room. He may have looked around to see if anyone was watching, anyone who might recognize him, then go outside to wait for him, to kill him.

The officer told him to sit down.

"What are you reporting?" the officer asked, pulling out a form from a folder on top of a desk already cluttered with piles and piles of papers. The officer grabbed a pen from under another set of papers and readied himself to write.

At the top of the form were the words:

POLICE NATIONALE D'HAITI
SERVICE D'IVESTIGATION ET ANTI-GANG (SIAG)
SECTION DE DOLEANCES

The last line indicated that my uncle was in the grievance section of the national police's investigation and anti-gang unit. And as if to remove any hope that the matter he was complaining about might actually be looked into, the word "investigation" was misspelled on the department letterhead.

The nature of the incident in question was summarized as "pillaging, theft and incineration." My uncle's declaration to the officer recounted what had happened that Sunday at the church as well as the following day. Among the many things he said he lost were "nos papiers importants," our important papers. He was asked to pay the officer forty Haitian dollars, the equivalent of five American dollars, for a photocopy of the original document, which the officer then laid on top of another large pile of such documents on his desk.

Could someone be sent to his house in Bel Air now to examine the situation? my uncle asked.

The officer said it was a bad time. They were too busy, but they would look into it later.

What about a justice of the peace, an examining judge, or an investigative judge, who was usually sent to the scene of a crime?

If he could find one to go at his own expense, the officer

said, he was welcome to send one there, but good luck to him, since no one was going into Bel Air right now, including CIMO officers and the UN.

But if the gangs took over his compound and he needed to eventually get it back, wouldn't he need a report from a justice of the peace?

"We're in a war now," the officer calmly explained. "We'll see what happens after the war."

But how much longer could this war go on? How many more would have to flee? How many would have to die? Wasn't the UN, the MINUSTAH, there to help end the war?

How could he file a similar report with the UN about the MINUSTAH? he asked.

The officer told him to go up to Bourdon, a small neighborhood up the hill, on the road leading to Pétion Ville, one of the city's suburbs. The headquarters of CIVPOL, the United Nations' Civilian Police Unit, were housed at the Villa Saint Louis, a twenty-five-room, sixty-U.S.-dollar-a-night hotel with spacious balconies overlooking parts of Port-au-Prince.

He left the anti-gang unit around noon, carrying his copy of the police report. It was scorching outside and he could feel the sun warm his face through the fuzz of a short beard that had grown there these last couple of days. He hadn't had a chance to shave at Man Jou's. He'd have to remember to buy a razor before he went to Tante Zi's so he could be clean-shaven for his flight the next day.

He then took another taxi to the Villa Saint Louis. At the entrance, he asked some soldiers in camouflage where he might file a complaint. The soldiers shrugged, not speaking any Creole or French.

"Português," they said, motioning for him to go farther inside.

In contrast to Bel Air and the anti-gang unit, the hotel seemed extremely luxurious with its swimming pool and sundeck, crowded with umbrella-topped tables. Before the raids began, he'd heard some of his parishioners joke that the MINUSTAH were actually TURISTA, tourists on an adventurous exploration. He wondered what these parishioners would say now if they could see this hotel.

Milling around the bar and lounge area were a large number of CIVPOL officers. As bewildering as life had suddenly become, there were now all these acronyms to remember. CIMO. SIAG. MINUSTAH. CIVPOL.

Unlike the MINUSTAH "peacekeepers" or soldiers, the CIVPOL officers all wore the uniforms of their own countries' police force with blue UN helmets and matching bulletproof vests. My uncle quickly recognized the scarlet tunic and breeches of the Royal Canadian Mounted Police French-speaking officers, who seemed to outnumber the other groups chatting in several different languages around him.

Approaching one, he asked in French if he could file a complaint.

The officer had trouble understanding his machine, so he had to repeat himself several times. The officer, a man whose face seemed as red as his tunic, perhaps from sunburn, took him aside to a quiet corner near a staircase, and as his eyes wandered toward some other officers having lunch around the pool, my uncle tried to tell him what had happened.

Had he filed a report at the anti-gang unit? the officer asked.

He answered yes and handed the SIAG report to the officer.

The officer took the report to him and told him to wait. He was going to make a copy.

The hum of multilingual chatter momentarily distracted my uncle as he waited. Soon the officer was back. He'd made a copy of the report, he said.

"Merci," my uncle said, not even certain himself why he was saying thank you.

Would some action be taken? my uncle asked. Would the UN soldiers who'd shot from his roof be disciplined? Would the people who'd been wounded be helped? Would the Red Cross go in and take them to the hospital? Would the families of the dead be compensated? Or at least assisted with funeral expenses?

It was likely that Haitian police officers had shot from his roof, the officer said. MINUSTAH and CIVPOL were simply there to assist the Haitian police. If his neighbors were wounded and killed by Haitian police, there was nothing the UN could do.

Had my uncle contacted any Haitian human rights organizations? he asked. The Haiti branch of the New York–based National Coalition for Haitian Rights, la Comité des Avocats pour le Respect des Libertés Individuelles or the Lawyers Committee for the Respect of Individual Rights?

He didn't know where these groups were located, my uncle said. Besides, he was leaving the country the next day. He must have realized how arrogant that must have sounded, how privileged, how lucky. There were so many others who were indefinitely trapped in the crossfire between the police and the UN and the gangs. He planned to come back, he said, which is why he wanted to have all these reports filed, so he could have his place back, live again where he had spent most of his life.

Good luck, the officer said.

Later, after leaving Léogâne and before going to Tante Zi's, Maxo would travel the same path as his father, neither one knowing that the other had gone to the anti-gang unit to file a report that he'd then carried to the UN. Maxo had gone to another building near the Villa Saint Louis Hotel, a place that also housed some UN offices. There he ran into more Brazilian officers and more corporals with the Royal Canadian Mounted Police. These men (there were very few women among these forces), and everyone else who wore a uniform, wielded a baton and carried a gun, inspired both awe and fear in Maxo and my uncle, for they were part of a constant pull and release, or what my uncle might have in Creole called "mòde soufle," where those who are most able to obliterate you are also the only ones offering some illusion of shelter and protection, a shred of hope—even if false—for possible restoration. In Maxo's SIAG report, as part of his "declaration de perte," or declaration of losses, he too listed "nos papiers importants," birth certificates, old report cards, family photos, school diplomas, the kind of things one might need to restore even the smallest fragments of a life.

I only learned of my uncle's predicament that Thursday night. Tante Zi had called her daughter in New York, who had passed the news on to my father.

During our nightly phone conversation, my father calmly

said, "You're pregnant, so don't upset yourself too much, but your uncle's had some problems in Bel Air."

"What happened?" I asked.

"I don't know all the details myself, but I hear there's a gang in his house right now."

"Where is *he*?" I asked.

"He and Maxo are at Zi's house. They're coming to Miami tomorrow. You'll see them before any of us will."

After sharing the news with my husband, I called Tante Zi's cell phone. In her usual exuberant way, in things both good and bad, Tante Zi detailed as much of the story as she knew, as much as my uncle had told her.

I asked her if I could speak to my uncle.

"He's asleep," she said.

"Maxo?"

"Him too."

She didn't have the heart to wake them, she said, because they'd been through so much and had slept so little these past few days, plus they had to get up early the next morning to catch their flight.

"Please tell them to call me in the morning," I said. "Tell them my husband and I want to know what flight they're on so we can pick them up."

One of my uncle's minister friends was picking them up, she said. My uncle had already arranged it. "Don't worry," she said. "They'll call you when they get there."

No Greater Shame

The next day, Friday, my father's health took a turn for the worse. Worried about my uncle, he hadn't slept the night before. His voice was so hoarse from coughing that he could barely speak when I called. His eczema and psoriasis had returned and he'd completely lost what little appetite he had.

My daughter had just begun to kick at night and her fetal acrobatics left me totally exhausted in the morning. I was in bed fighting a fainting spell when Bob called to tell me about Papa.

"Maybe you should take him to the hospital," I told Bob.

"He doesn't want to go," Bob said. "He says they'll just send him home like all the other times."

As Bob spoke, I could hear my father coughing and moaning loudly in the background.

"He's getting worse," Bob added. "And this thing with Uncle's not helping."

I wanted very much to be in New York with my father,

so I closed my eyes and imagined myself there. I am sitting on the edge of his bed and we're watching my father's favorite game show, *The Price Is Right,* on television. Unsure of the answers, we guess wildly but still get all of them right anyway. This makes my father so happy that he rises out of bed and starts to dance. At first he dances like a ballerina in slow motion, but then he increases his pace, until he's jumping up and down, bouncing on and off his bed.

When I woke up, I wasn't sure whether this was reverie or dream. However, when I looked at the digital clock on my bedside table, it was after three p.m.

The phone was ringing, which is why I'd woken up in the first place. I picked it up, expecting my uncle and Maxo. Instead it was Tante Zi.

"Are they with you?" she asked.

"Non," I said.

Perhaps they'd called and I'd missed them. I looked for the flashing message button on the phone. The call log also registered no calls.

"Their plane should have landed by now," Tante Zi said. They'd gone to the airport very early, but their plane had left sometime after noon.

"I took them to the airport myself." She was speaking loud and fast. There was an edginess to her voice, a strain of anxiety. "I took them in a camionette.

"I sent you tablèt," she added, "the kind I know you like. "Uncle has them for you."

That she remembered to send me some peanut confections at such a stressful time amazed me.

"I thought you might have some cravings," she said. "Unsatisfied cravings can lead to birthmarks on the baby."

She was quiet for a moment, then started again in the same quick and loud voice.

"Listen, take good care of your uncle," she said. "He's lost everything."

"I'll take care of him," I said.

"I don't think he should come back to Haiti for a long time," she continued. "It's crazy here now. No peace."

I attributed the fact that I didn't hear from my uncle and Maxo to a plane delay. Then I called the airline, American Airlines, and found out that the plane my uncle and Maxo had meant to be on had left and landed. Because of privacy laws, they couldn't tell me whether my uncle and Maxo had been on it or not. As it got later and my husband returned from work, I grew increasingly nervous. Maybe they'd missed their plane altogether, my husband said, and were bumped to the next day.

The early evening went by with no news. Then more calls, first from Uncle Franck in New York, then from my father. Worrying me even more, my uncle's pastor friend also called. His wife had waited three hours at Miami International Airport and had seen no sign of either my uncle or Maxo.

Around nine p.m., the calls suddenly stopped. Cell phones in tow, Fedo and I went for what we'd come to call our daily pregnancy walk on the boardwalk on Miami Beach. It was a balmy night, but a cool breeze was coming off the ocean. We didn't walk long. Worried that my uncle might remember only the house telephone number, we hurried home to wait by the phone. Intermittently, I called Tante Zi on her cell phone, but I got no reply.

Fedo and I lay down and tried to brainstorm some possibilities. I wanted to have at least one likely explanation for my father.

"They're probably coming tomorrow," I told my father when he called.

My father had merely called to check on my uncle and Maxo. He was too weak to continue talking. I fell into a deep, sad sleep.

My phone rang at one thirty the next morning. Ever since my father had become ill, late-night and early-morning phone calls sent my now very large body leaping straight out of bed. Still, I missed the call.

On the voice mail was a message from a female U.S. Customs and Border Protection officer. She could have read from a Contact Advisory of CBP Detention form, which contains a script provided by Customs and Border Protection that would have had her say, "I am Officer So-and-so of U.S Customs and Border Protection at Miami International Airport. Your uncle, who has arrived in the United States on American Airlines flight 822, has asked that we contact you . . ." However, what she said instead was "Ms. Danticat, we have your uncle here."

She then paused, and it sounded as though she moved her mouth slightly away from the phone to ask my uncle, "What is your name, sir?"

My uncle's voice box came through clearly as he replied, "Joseph Dantica." He pronounced his name in the French way, putting the most emphasis on the last syllable. Though an error on my father's birth certificate had made him a Danticat, giving us a singular variation of the family name, we still pronounced our surnames the same. In French and Cre-ole our *t* was silent, though I often joked with my uncle that in English we were "cats" and he was not.

"We have him here," the female officer continued on the message, "at U.S. Customs and Border Protection. He's re-quested asylum and we're completing his paperwork."

There was hope, kindness in her voice, a matter-of-fact impression of normalcy and routine. But her number had not registered on my phone, and she hadn't left it for me to call back.

My husband searched the Internet while I leafed through the Yellow Pages for a Customs and Border Protection listing at Miami International Airport. After a while we got through.

"Someone just called me," I said. "About an elderly man and his son."

"I'm familiar with them," the man who replied said. In his few words, I could hear the disdain, which perhaps was always in his voice, but seemed nevertheless particularly directed at me. "They came here with no papers and tried to get in—"

"They have papers," I tried to explain.

"I'm sorry," he said, "but I have two flights coming in." Then he hung up.

"We have to go to the airport," I told my husband. We were only fifteen minutes away and were not getting anywhere on the phone.

At the closed American Airlines counter at the airport, we found a Haitian janitor who directed us to the entrance to the Customs and Border Protection offices. They too were closed. Standing outside the metal doors, I dialed the offices' number again.

Another male officer picked up.

"Someone called me," I said, "about my uncle, Joseph Dantica. He should be with his son, Maxo."

"They're right here in front of me." This was the kindest and most polite-sounding voice yet.

"I'm in the airport," I said.

"Yes?"

"I've come to pick them up."

His long pause indicated some kind of misunderstanding on my part. Something had been said to me that I'd obviously not fully grasped.

"We only called to notify you that they're here," he said. "They're not being released. They're going to Krome."

My heart sank. The year before, I had been to the Krome detention center as part of a delegation of community observers organized by the Florida Immigrant Advocacy Center. A series of gray concrete buildings and trailers, Krome was out in what seemed like the middle of nowhere, in southwest Miami. During our visit, a group of men in identical dark blue overalls had been escorted into a covered, chain-link-fenced, concrete patio rimmed by rows of barbed wire. The men walked in two straight lines, sat at the long cafeteria-style tables and told our delegation their stories. They were Haitian "boat people" and in addition to their names identified themselves by the vessels on which they'd come.

"My name is . . . ," they said. "I came on the July boat." Or "I came on the December boat."

Some invented parables to explain their circumstances.

One man spoke of mad dogs—gang members—threatening him and forcing him to seek shelter at a neighbor's house, the neighbor being the United States. Another sang about a mud slide, meaning the Lavalas or Flood Party, that had washed everything away. Another asked us to tell the world the detainees were beaten sometimes. He told of a friend who'd had his back broken by a guard and was deported before he could get medical attention. Some detainees fought among themselves, sometimes nearly killing each other as uninterested guards looked on. They spoke of other guards who told them they smelled, who taunted them while telling them that unlike the Cuban rafters, who were guaranteed refuge, they would never get asylum, that few Haitians ever get asylum. They said that the large rooms where they slept in rows and rows of bunk beds were often so overcrowded that some of them had to sleep on thin mattresses on the floor. They were at times so cold that they shivered all night long. They told of the food that rather than nourish them, punished them, gave them diarrhea and made them vomit. They told of arbitrary curfews, how they were woken up at six a.m. and forced to go back to that cold room by six p.m.

I'd seen some men who looked too young to be the mandatory eighteen years old for detention at Krome. A few of them looked fourteen or even twelve. How can we be sure they're not younger, I'd asked one of the lawyers in our delegation, if they come with no birth certificates, no papers? The lawyer answered that their ages were determined by examining their teeth. I couldn't escape this agonizing reminder of slavery auction blocks, where mouths were pried open to determine worth and state of health.

One man, who had received asylum but had not yet been released when we visited, showed us burn marks over his arms, chest and belly. His flesh was seared white, with rows and rows of keloid scars. It seemed like such a violation, to look at his belly, the space where the scars dipped farther down his body. But he was used to showing his scars, he said. He had to show them to a number of immigration judges to prove he deserved to stay.

I'd sat across from an older man, a man who looked like he might be around my father's age, who'd said, "If I had a bullet, I'd have shot myself already. I'm not a criminal. I'm not used to prison."

The shame of being a prisoner loomed large. A stigma most couldn't shake. To have been shackled, handcuffed, many said, rubbing that spot on their wrists where the soft manacles were placed on them soon after they made it to the American shore, "I have known no greater shame in my life."

I'd met a young man from Bel Air. His eyes were red. He couldn't stop crying. His mother had died the week before, he said, and he couldn't even attend her funeral. He told me his mother's name, and when he described her house, the house where he used to live in Bel Air, I could see it. It was not far from my uncle's house.

"Can I speak to my uncle?" I asked the customs officer, who, it seemed, was patiently waiting for me to get off the phone.

"That's not allowed," he said.

"Please," I said. "He's old and—"

"He'll contact you when he gets to Krome."

Alien 27041999

My uncle was now alien 27041999. He and Maxo had left Port-au-Prince's Toussaint Louverture Airport on American Airlines flight 822. The flight was scheduled to leave at 12:32 p.m., but was a bit delayed and left later than that.

On the plane, my uncle attempted to write a narrative of what had happened to him on a piece of white paper. He titled his note "Epidemie du 24 octobre 2004."

"Un groupe de chimères ont détruit L'Eglise Chrétienne de la Rédemption," it began. "A group of chimères destroyed Eglise Chrétienne de la Redemption." He then gave up writing sentences to simply list what had been removed or burned from the church, including the pews, two padded ballroom chairs used at wedding ceremonies, a drum set, some speakers and microphones.

Once they got off the plane at around two thirty p.m., my uncle and Maxo waited their turn with a large group of visitors in one of the long Customs and Border Protection lines.

When they reached the CBP checkpoint, they presented their passports and valid tourist visas to a CPB officer. When asked how long they would be staying in the United States, my uncle, not understanding the full implication of that choice, said he wanted to apply for temporary asylum. He and Maxo were then taken aside and placed in a customs waiting area.

I don't know why my uncle had not simply used the valid visa he had to enter the United States, just as he had at least thirty times before, and later apply for asylum. I'm sure now that he had no intention of staying in either New York or Miami for the rest of his life. This is why, according to Maxo, he had specified "temporary." Had he acted based on someone's advice? On something he'd heard on the radio, read in the newspapers? Did he think that given all that had happened to him, the authorities—again those with the power both to lend a hand and to cut one off—would have to believe him? He planned to stay at most a few weeks, a few months, but he was determined to go back. This was why he'd gotten his police report from the anti-gang unit. This was why he had wanted the officer, a justice of the peace or an investigative judge, to go to Bel Air to witness and inspect, so he could return when things were calmer and reclaim his house, school and church. He had said as much to Tante Zi the day before.

I can only assume that when he was asked how long he would be staying in the United States, he knew that he would be staying past the thirty days his visa allowed him and he wanted to tell the truth.

. . .

Maxo and my uncle were approached by another Customs and Border Protection officer again at 5:38 p.m., at which point it was determined that my uncle would need a translator for his interview. Maxo, a fluent English speaker, could not as his son act as his translator.

Documents from the Bureau of Customs and Border Protection indicate that my uncle was interviewed by an Officer Reyes with help from a translator. A standard CBP interview form would have had Officer Reyes begin by saying, "I am an officer of the United States Immigration and Naturalization Service. I am authorized to administer the immigration laws and take sworn statements. I want to take your sworn statement regarding your application for admission to the United States."

A digitized picture attached to my uncle's interview form shows him looking tired and perplexed. His head is cropped from the tip of his widow's peak down to his chin. The picture shows a bit of his shoulder, which is slumped back, away from the frame. He is wearing a jacket, the same one that, according to Maxo, he'd been wearing since he left his house in Bel Air. Though he is facing the camera, his eyes are turned sideways, possibly toward the photographer.

The interview began with Officer Reyes asking my uncle, "Do you understand what I have said to you?"

"Yes," answered my uncle.

"Are you willing to answer my questions at this time?"

After making my uncle swear and affirm that all the statements he was about to make would be true and complete, Officer Reyes asked him to state his full name.

"Dantica Joseph Nosius," answered my uncle.

"Of what country are you a citizen?"

"Haiti."

"Do you have any reason to believe you are a citizen of the United States?"

"NO."

"Do you have any family, mother, father, brother, sister, spouse, or child who are citizens or permanent residents of the United States?"

My uncle replied that he had two brothers in the United States, one—my father—a naturalized U.S. citizen, and the second—my uncle Franck—a permanent resident.

"What is your purpose in entering the United States today?" asked Officer Reyes.

"Because a group that is causing trouble in Haiti wants to kill me," my uncle answered.

According to the transcript, Officer Reyes did not ask for further explanation or details.

"How much money do you have?" he asked, proceeding with the interview.

My uncle answered that he had one thousand and nine U.S. dollars with him.

"What is your occupation?" asked Officer Reyes.

The transcriber/translator has my uncle saying, "I am a priest," but he most likely said he was an evèk, a bishop, or elder pastor.

"What documents did you present today to the first Customs and Border Protection officer that you encountered?" asked Officer Reyes.

"My Haitian passport and immigration forms," my uncle answered.

"What name is on those documents?"

"Dantica Joseph Nosius."

"Is the name on the documents your true and correct name?"

"Yes."

"Have you ever used any other names?"

"No."

"Are you currently taking any prescription medication for any health condition?" asked Officer Reyes.

The transcriber/translator has my uncle saying, "Yes, for back pain and chest." And in parentheses, writes, "ibuprofen."

The transcript has neither my uncle nor the interviewer mentioning two rum bottles filled with herbal medicine, one for himself and one for my father, as well as the smaller bottles of prescription pills he was taking for his blood pressure and inflamed prostate.

"How would you describe your current health status?" Officer Reyes continued.

According to the transcript, my uncle answered, "Not bad." He had probably said, "Pa pi mal," just as my father continued to, even as he lay dying.

"Have you ever been arrested before at any time or any place?"

"No."

"Why exactly are you requesting for [sic] political asylum in the United States today?"

"Because they burned down my church in Haiti and I fear for my life."

Again no further explanation or details were requested and my uncle did not offer more.

"Have you had [sic] applied for political asylum before in the United States or any other country?"

"No."

"Have anyone [sic] ever petition for you to become a United States Legal Permanent Resident"

"No."

"Were you in the United States in the year 1984?"

"Yes, but I do not remember."

(I couldn't remember either whether or not he'd been in the United States in 1984. I knew he had been the year before, during the summer of 1983, when he got the voice box, but could not recall if he'd returned the following year.)

"Have you have any encounter [sic] the United States Immigration Services before?"

"No."

"Why did you leave your home country of last residence?"

"Because I fear for my life in Haiti. And they burned down my church."

"Do you have any fear or concern about being returned to your home country or being removed from the United States?"

"Yes."

"Would you be harmed if you are returned to your home country of last residence?"

"YES."

"Did you understand my questions?"

"Yes."

"Do you have any questions or is there anything you'd like to add?"

"No."

My uncle was then asked to sign the statement. He was supposed to have initialed each page of the translated transcript, but instead he signed his name on all five pages. A CBP log shows he was then returned to the waiting area, where at 7:40 p.m. he was given some soda and chips.

At 10:03 p.m., my uncle Franck received a call at his home in Brooklyn. The male CBP officer who called him asked Uncle Franck whether Uncle Joseph had filed an application to become a U.S. resident in 1984. Uncle Franck said no.

Later, Department of Homeland Security files would show that a September 22, 1983, request had been made by Kings County Hospital, where my uncle had had his surgery and subsequent follow-up visits, to the United States Department of Justice, about my uncle's immigration status. As a result of this, on February 14, 1984, an immigration "alien" file, number 27041999, a file he was never aware of, was opened for my uncle. The file was subsequently closed.

"He's been coming to the United States for more than thirty years," Uncle Franck remembers telling the CPB officer who called him. "If he wanted to stay, he would have stayed a long time ago."

Uncle Franck then asked if he could speak to Uncle Joseph.

"They say they're going to put me in prison," Uncle Franck remembers Uncle Joseph saying. It was difficult to register emotion on the voice box, but Uncle Franck thought he sounded like he was caught up in something he had no way of understanding.

"It's not true. They can't put you in prison," Uncle Franck

recalls telling him. "You have a visa. You have papers. Did you tell them how long you've been coming here?"

Uncle Franck then asked Uncle Joseph to put the CBP officer on the phone again.

"He's going to Krome," the officer said.

"He can't," Uncle Franck said. "He's eighty-one years old, an old man."

Uncle Franck then asked if he could speak to my uncle one more time.

The CBP officer told him, "We already have a translator for him," and hung up.

At 11:00 p.m., my uncle was given some chips and soda again. At 11:45 p.m., he signed a form saying his personal property was returned to him. The form lists as personal property only his one thousand and nine dollars and a silver-colored wristwatch. At 1:30 a.m., I received my phone call. At 4:20 a.m., my uncle and Maxo were transported to the airport's satellite detention area, which was in another concourse. By then my uncle was so cold that he wrapped the woolen airplane blanket he was given tightly around him as he curled up in a fetal position on a cement bed until 7:15 a.m. At around 7:30 a.m., they left the detention area to board a white van to Krome. Maxo was handcuffed, but asked if my uncle could not be handcuffed because of his age. The officer agreed not to handcuff my uncle, but told Maxo to tell my uncle that if he tried to escape he would be shot.

There is a form called a Discretionary Authority Checklist for Alien Applicants, which is meant to assist examining Customs and Border Protection officers in deciding whether to detain or release a person like my uncle. On the checklist are questions such as: Does the alien pose a threat to the United States, have a criminal history or terrorist affiliations or ties? Is s/he likely to contribute to the illegal population or pose some other credible threat?

Noting the "nature" of my uncle's inadmissibility, Officer Reyes cited a positive Central Index System search involving the February 14, 1984 immigration file and alien number.

In the remarks section beneath his check mark, he wrote, "Subject has an A#" or an alien registration number. In a more detailed memo, he would later write, "The Central Index System revealed that subject had an existing A (27041999) number which revealed negative results to him being a resident. The Central Index System did not contain any information on the subject except his name and date of birth and activity date of 02/14/1984."

Still, I suspect that my uncle was treated according to a biased immigration policy dating back from the early 1980s when Haitians began arriving in Florida in large numbers by boat. In Florida, where Cuban refugees are, as long as they're able to step foot on dry land, immediately processed and released to their families, Haitian asylum seekers are disproportionately detained, then deported. While Hondurans and Nicaraguans have continued to receive protected status for nearly ten years since Hurricane Mitch struck their homelands, Haitians were deported to the flood zones weeks after Tropical Storm Jeanne blanketed an entire city in water the way Hurricane Katrina did parts of New Orleans. Was my uncle going to jail because he was Haitian? This is a question he probably asked himself. This is a question I still ask myself. Was he going to jail because he was black? If he were white, Cuban, anything other than Haitian, would he have been going to Krome?

"Are age and health factors in this situation?" demands the Discretionary Authority Checklist for Alien Applicants.

In spite of my uncle's eighty-one years and his being a survivor of throat cancer, which was obvious from his voice box and tracheotomy, when answering whether there were age and health factors to be taken into consideration, Officer Reyes checked No.

Is the applicant a well-known public figure?

No.

Congressional or media interest?

No.

Does the applicant have a legitimate reason for entering the U.S.?

No.

Is the applicant's reason for entry based on an emergency?

No.

Credible claim of official misinformation?

No.

Is there a relationship to a U.S. employer or resident?

Yes.

Intent to circumvent admissibility requirements?

No.

Misrepresentations made by applicant during inspection process?

No.

Would the applicant be admissible if s/he had a valid passport and/or visa? (My uncle had both.)

Yes.

Is there relief for the applicant through the parole or visa waiver process?

No.

Tomorrow

My father's rough patch had continued. He was becoming agitated, panicked at times over his decreasing ability to speak for extended periods. His anxiety sent us on a renewed search. During his monthly visit with Dr. Padman, Bob asked if he could be considered for any experimental treatment programs and procured a referral to a pulmonologist at Columbia Presbyterian in upper Manhattan.

Suddenly my father had a place and time on which to pin his hopes. He was so looking forward to his appointment that he would end each of our brief conversations by saying, "We'll see what they tell me at Columbia."

On Saturday morning, as my father struggled for breath and dreamed of Columbia, I had to tell him that his brother was at Krome, a place that he, like all Haitians, knew meant nothing less than humiliation and suffering and more often than not a long period of detention before deportation.

"So it's true," he said. Uncle Franck had called the night before to tell him that Uncle Joseph might be going there.

"I hate to put this on you," my father said. "You're pregnant, but you're the only family he has down there. It's in your hands."

I told him that Fedo and I had already called a few immigration lawyers and they'd all advised us that there was nothing we could do before Monday morning.

"You mean," my father said, "Uncle has to spend the whole weekend in jail?"

When he arrived at Krome, my uncle was lined up with a dozen or so other detainees and his briefcase inventoried and taken away from him. A Krome property inventory form lists one softcover religious book, his Bible, one thousand U.S. dollars—he was allowed to keep the nine dollars to buy phone cards—one airline ticket, one tube of Fixodent for his dentures, and two nine-volt batteries for his two voice boxes. Again there's no mention of the herbal medicine or the pills he was taking for his blood pressure and inflamed prostate.

My uncle's initial medical screening involved an examination of his vital signs, chest X-rays, and a physical and mental history interview. In the notes jotted down by the examining nurse, he is described as composed, friendly and "purposeful." To the question "Does the detainee understand and recognize the significance and symptoms of the situation in which he finds himself?" the nurse answers, "Yes," adding elsewhere, "Patient uses a traditional Haitian medicine for prostate & says if he doesn't take it he pees blood & has pain." Russ Knocke, a spokesman for U.S. Immigration and Customs Enforcement, would later derogatorily refer to my uncle's traditional medicine as "a voodoolike potion."

At the end of his first day at Krome, my uncle's blood pressure was so high that he was assigned to the Short Stay Unit, a medical facility inside the prison. He and Maxo were separated.

I am acquainted with Ira Kurzban, author of *Kurzban's Immigration Law Sourcebook,* one of the most widely used immigration manuals in the United States. Ira had represented Haitian immigrant clients for more than thirty years and had worked as general counsel to the governments of Panama, Nicaragua, Cuba and Haiti and as former president Aristide's attorney. On the recommendation of a mutual friend, I called his office early Monday morning and asked for his help.

"I'm sending one of my best guys on this," he said, after I explained the entire situation to him. "Because of his age and health condition, we'll first try to get your uncle out as soon as possible."

Soon after Ira hung up, John Pratt, a stern-sounding man with a slight southern drawl, called.

"I'm heading to Krome now," he said. "I'll need as much information as you have about the situation."

I told him all I knew. I hadn't been able to speak to my uncle since his arrival, so I couldn't offer much insight into his state of mind or how he might come across at a credible fear hearing, an inquiry into his claims of persecution that would be held before an asylum officer at Krome.

"Are you willing to take him in if they release him?" Pratt asked.

"Of course," I said.

"Hang on tight then and stay by the phone," he said.

Once there was only waiting to do, my husband left for work. I called some Brooklyn ambulette companies about transporting my father to Columbia Presbyterian the next day. My father had so little fat and muscle left on his body that it was agonizing for him to sit for any stretch of time, so I basically wanted to rent him a bed on wheels.

"The only way you get a bed is if you call 911," a Russian dispatcher told me, so I booked a van with a recliner.

All morning, I hoped that John Pratt would call and tell me he was going to walk out of Krome with my uncle, news I would have loved to share with my father. However, when Pratt did call that afternoon the only good news was that my uncle's credible fear hearing had been scheduled for nine o'clock the next morning.

"So he's not coming home?" I said. Even as I said it, the word "home" felt inappropriate, unsuitable. My uncle no longer had a home.

"Can I visit him?" I asked.

"Only weekend visits are allowed at Krome," he said, "and he'd have to put you on a list a couple of days before the fact, but there's a good chance they'll release him tomorrow."

That night at around six o'clock, my uncle called me from Krome.

"Bon dye," I shouted, so overjoyed to hear that motorized voice. "My God. It's so good to hear you."

"Oh, I can't tell you how good it is to hear you," he said.

Then I slipped into a repartee I had fallen into with my

father in the last weeks or so as he'd grown sicker. I called him cher, amour, mon coeur, darling, my love, my heart.

"How are you, my heart?"

"M nan prizon," he said. I'm in jail.

"Oh I know," I said, now missing his real voice, the one that didn't always sound the same, the one I could no longer fully remember. "I know and I am so sad. I'm so sad and sorry for everything that's happened both in Haiti and here. But you met with the lawyer?"

"Yes," he said. "Maxo and I both did."

"He's going to get you out," I said. "He's a very good lawyer. He's going to get you out."

"Okay," he said. He'd had so many horrible surprises in the last few days, why should he believe that things would start going well now?

"Nèg nan prizon," he said. "Fò w mache pou wè." If you live long enough you'll see everything.

"Don't worry," I said. "We'll get you out."

"They took my medicine." The machine produced some static as if his finger had slipped off the button that he pressed to keep the voice going. "I also had something for your father, some liquid vitamins. They took that too. And my papers, my notepads, they're gone. Burned."

"Don't worry about all that," I said. "Just concentrate on getting out tomorrow."

"Does he know?" he asked. "Does Mira know I'm in here? I didn't want him to know. He's so sick. I don't want him to have this on his mind."

"Don't worry," I said. "He knows you're getting out tomorrow."

"Do people in Haiti know?" he asked. He was most concerned about his sisters, Tante Zi and Tante Tina.

"I think they know," I said.

Now even the motorized voice betrayed a hint of shame, the kind of shame whose only reprieve is silence.

"I have to go," he said. "Others are waiting."

"How do you feel?" I asked. "If you don't feel well, tell them."

"I will," he said. "I have to go."

I heard a muffled voice in the background, someone demanding a turn at the pay phone.

"You're strong," I said. "Very strong. You have so much more strength than even you know."

And reluctantly he agreed and said, "Oh yes. It's true."

"Just get through tonight," I said. "Tomorrow, God willing, you'll be free."

Afflictions

My father every now and then would quote from the book of Genesis, paraphrasing his favorite lines from the story of Joseph, the youth who was ousted and sold into unfriendly territory by his brothers. My uncle Joseph was named after the rainbow-coated man, but I'd never heard Papa look for parallels between my uncle's life and the biblical story before.

"Uncle is in his own Egypt this morning, in his land of afflictions," my father said, when we talked just before nine a.m. the next day.

"He's going to be all right," I said. "You just concentrate on Columbia Presbyterian."

As I was talking to my father, my uncle was waiting with John Pratt outside an asylum unit trailer office at Krome. Leaning over to one of three other detainees also waiting for hearings, my uncle asked the English-speaking Haitian man to tell Pratt that his medication had been taken away. Before Pratt could respond, he and my uncle were called in by asylum officer Castro, a woman who appeared to be in her mid-forties. The asylum interview was about to begin.

My uncle and Pratt were seated at a desk close to the back wall, facing Officer Castro. A certified translator was needed for the proceedings, and since there wasn't one on the premises, a telephone translation service was called and the interpreter put on speakerphone. The phone was on the desk in front of my uncle, next to Pratt's lawbooks, notepads and other materials.

The interpreter had trouble understanding my uncle's voice box, so Officer Castro asked my uncle to move his mouth closer to the phone. As my uncle leaned forward, his hand slipped away from his neck and he dropped his voice box.

The records indicate that my uncle appeared to be having a seizure. His body stiffened. His legs jerked forward. His chair slipped back, pounding the back of his head into the wall. He began to vomit.

Vomit shot out of his mouth, his nose, as well as the tracheotomy hole in his neck. The vomit was spread all over his face, from his forehead to his chin, down the front of his dark blue Krome-issued overalls. There was also vomit on his thighs, where a large wet stain showed he had also urinated on himself.

"Somebody call for help!" Pratt jumped from his chair and pulled his papers away from the spreading vomit.

Officer Castro rushed over to the desk and grabbed the sleeves of my uncle's uniform. She pulled his body forward, straightening his head. Grabbing a nearby wastebasket, she placed it in front of my uncle. My uncle continued to vomit into the wastebasket as he opened and closed his eyes, which wandered aimlessly in their sockets.

When he stopped vomiting, my uncle's body grew rigid and cold, his arms falling limply at his side. Officer Castro called out to the guards keeping watch over the other detainees outside her office and asked them to call the medical unit. A guard radioed for help but said that Krome was in lockdown and that it might take some time for help to arrive.

Officer Castro grabbed the phone in front of my uncle to see if the interpreter was still there. The phone was dead. She asked if there was anyone around who could speak to my uncle in Creole. The guard brought the English-speaking Haitian detainee to whom my uncle had spoken about his medication into the asylum office. The man said a few words to my uncle, but there was no reaction. Pratt asked Officer Castro to send for Maxo. The guard said he needed special permission from his supervisor to have Maxo come. The guard radioed for special permission.

Fifteen minutes had passed since my uncle first started vomiting. A registered nurse and medic finally arrived. By then my uncle looked "almost comatose," Pratt recalled. "He seemed somewhat unconscious and couldn't move."

Pratt told the medic and nurse that right before he became sick, my uncle had told him his medication had been taken away. Pratt then turned to Officer Castro and asked if my uncle could be granted humanitarian parole given his age and condition.

"I think he's faking," the medic said, cutting Pratt off.

To prove his point, the medic grabbed my uncle's head and moved it up and down. It was rigid rather than limp, he said. Besides, my uncle would open his eyes now and then and seemed to be looking at him.

"You can't fake vomit," Pratt shot back. "This man is very sick and his medication shouldn't have been taken away from him."

The medications were indeed taken away, replied the medic, in accordance with the facility's regulations, and others were substituted for them.

The medic and the nurse then moved my uncle from the asylum office to a wheelchair in the hallway.

When Maxo arrived, he ran over to his father and seeing him slumped over in the wheelchair and leaning over the side, began to cry. Except for the occasional flutter of his eyelids, it seemed to Maxo that his father was unconscious. The first thing Maxo wanted to do was clean the vomit from his face. Though his father was in distress, he knew that underneath the sticky heave and chunks of still undigested food, this very proud man would feel humiliated by his appearance.

"He wouldn't be like this if you hadn't taken away his medication," Maxo said, sobbing.

"He's faking," repeated the medic. "He keeps looking at me."

The medic then turned to Pratt and told him that based on his many years of experience at Krome, he could easily make such determinations.

"Please just let me clean him," Maxo sobbed.

The medic told him that he'd been called only to help his father communicate with them. "If you can't help, then we'll send you back."

"He can't speak without his voice box," Maxo said. Covered in vomit, the voice box was no longer operable.

During that discussion, it seemed to Maxo that his father's eyes were fluttering a bit more. Maybe he could hear them. Maybe he was getting better, coming out of whatever had overcome him.

"Papa," Maxo pleaded, "please try to move. Maybe they'll let you go."

My uncle opened his eyes and looked up at Maxo. He raised his hands from his lap, but they fell limply back to his knees. It seemed to Maxo that he was trying to mouth, "M pa kapab." I can't.

My uncle's eyes remained open, but they seemed cloudy and dazed, set on something way beyond Maxo, the guards, the medic, John Pratt and all the others around him.

"He's not cooperating," the medic said. For a moment Maxo wasn't sure whether the medic was talking about him or his father.

"His eyes are open and he's not unconscious," added the medic. "I still think he's faking, but we'll take him to the clinic."

A stretcher was brought and my uncle placed on it.

Pratt asked Officer Castro if they could continue the credible fear interview at the clinic.

No, he was told. That was against the rules.

I was on the phone with the medical transport service that was taking my father to Columbia Presbyterian when John Pratt called to tell me that my uncle had become ill. I was expecting good news, great news even. Before Pratt could even speak, I wanted to say, "Where do I go? How do I get him?"

"Your uncle became ill during the credible fear interview." Pratt's solid voice was shaken. There was even a hint of horror in it.

"They've taken him to the clinic at Krome," he said. "I'm in the lobby, waiting to see if we can continue the interview in a while. Mr. Kurzban is making calls to the Miami district office to see if your uncle can receive a humanitarian parole."

Later that morning, in the Krome medical unit, my uncle's condition worsened and according to Krome records, he was transported to Miami's Jackson Memorial Hospital with shackles on his feet. That same morning was the first time in nine weeks that my father had been out of his house. It was a crisp autumn day in New York and most of the leaves had already fallen off the trees. Speeding down the Prospect Expressway toward Manhattan, my father felt every stop and turn, every painful jolt and bounce of the ride in his bones. Still, between coughing spells, he told my mother and Bob, "At least I'm outside."

Being outside was all my father got out of the visit. The lung specialist who saw him made him take off his shirt, listened to his labored breathing, and asked him if he had a DNR.

"What's a DNR?" my father asked Bob in Creole.

"It's a piece of paper that says if you die, you don't want to be brought back to life and kept alive by machines," Bob explained.

"No," my father told the doctor. "I don't want to be kept alive by machines. There's already been enough suffering."

Let the Stars Fall

My uncle's medical records indicate that he arrived in the emergency room at Jackson Memorial Hospital around 1:00 p.m. with an intravenous drip in progress from Krome. He was evaluated by a nurse practitioner at 1:10 p.m., his pulse (80), temperature (97.0), blood pressure (169/78) checked and noted. At 2:00 p.m., he signed, in an apparently firm hand, a patient consent form stating, "I [he did not fill in his name in the blank spot] consent to undergo all necessary tests, medication, treatments and other procedures in the course of the study, diagnosis and treatment of my illness(es) by the medical staff and other agents and/or employees of the Public Health Trust/Jackson Memorial Hospital (PHT/JMH) and the University of Miami School of Medicine, including medical students."

At 3:24 p.m., blood and urine samples were taken. His urine analysis showed some blood and a high level of glucose. His CBC, or complete blood count test, displayed a higher than normal number of white blood cells, which hinted at a possible infection. The test also showed elevated bilirubin or abnormal gallbladder and liver functions.

At 4:00 p.m., during a more thorough evaluation by the nurse practitioner, he complained of acute abdominal pain, nausea and loss of appetite. A new IV was administered. Chest X-rays and abdominal films were taken. Pneumonia and intestinal obstruction were ruled out.

At 5 p.m., he was transferred to the hospital's prison area, Ward D. His Ward D admission note, which was also prepared by a registered nurse, remarks, "No acute distress, ambulatory. To IV hydrate and reevaluate. Patient closely observed."

Once in Ward D, where no lawyers or family members are allowed to visit, and where prisoners are restrained to prevent escapes, to protect the staff, the guards and the prisoners from one another, his feet were probably shackled once more, just as, according to Krome records, they'd been during the ambulance ride. He was given another IV at 10:00 p.m., at which time it was noted by the nurse on duty that he was "resting quietly." He was to be further observed and followed up, she added.

His vital signs were checked again at midnight, then at 1:00 a.m. and 7:00 a.m. the next day, when his temperature was 96 degrees, his heart rate a dangerous 114 beats per minute and his blood pressure 159/80. At 9:00 a.m. he was given another IV and 5 mg of Vasotec to help lower his blood pressure. By 11:00 a.m., his heart rate had decreased to 102 beats per minute, still distressingly high for an eighty-one-year-old man with his symptoms.

The records indicate that he was seen for the first time by

a physician at 1:00 p.m., exactly twenty-four hours after he'd been brought to the emergency room. The physician, Dr. Hernandez, noted his test results, namely his high white cell count, his elevated liver enzymes and his persistent abdominal pain. He then ordered an abdominal ultrasound, which was performed at 4:56 p.m. The ultrasound showed intra-abdominal fluid around my uncle's liver and sludge, or thickened bile, in his gallbladder. Before the test was administered, my uncle was given another patient consent form to sign. He signed it less comprehensibly than the first, next to a stamped hospital declaration of "PATIENT UNABLE TO SIGN."

At 7:00 p.m., after more than twenty hours of no food and sugarless IV fluids, my uncle was sweating profusely and complained of weakness. He was found to be hypoglycemic, with a lower than normal blood sugar level of 42 mg/dl. The doctor on duty prescribed a 5 percent dextrose drip and twenty minutes later, my uncle's blood glucose stabilized at 121 mg/dl. It was then noted that he was awake and alert and his mental response "appropriate."

At 7:55 p.m., his heart rate rose again, this time to 110 beats per minute. An electrocardiogram (EKG) was performed at 8:16 p.m. The next note on the chart shows that he was found pulseless and unresponsive by an immigration guard at 8:30 p.m. There is no detailed account of "the code" or the sixteen minutes between the time he was found unresponsive and the time he was pronounced dead, at 8:46 p.m. Only a quick scribble that cardiopulmonary resuscitation (CPR) and advanced cardiac life support (ACLS) "continued for 11mins."

. . .

Aside from the time he had throat cancer, my uncle nearly died on one other occasion. It was the summer of 1975, and I was six years old. He was stricken with malaria. Fever, chills, nausea and diarrhea had sent him to his doctor, who'd hospitalized him.

I hadn't seen him in several days when Tante Denise brought Nick, Bob and me to the hospital to visit him. When we walked into his small private room, he was curled in a fetal position, and though he was wrapped in several blankets, was shivering. His face was ashen and gray and his eyes the color of corn.

"The children are here," Tante Denise had told him.

He seemed not to see us. Grunting, he closed his eyes as if to protect them from the ache coursing through the rest of his body. When he opened his eyes again, he glared at us as if wondering what we were doing there.

"I brought the children," Tante Denise said again. "You asked for them."

He looked at each one of us carefully, then said, "Ti moun, children."

"Wi," we answered, a weak chorus of five- and six-year-olds.

Looking at Nick, my uncle said, "Maxo, I'll be sad to die without seeing you again." Then turning to Bob, he said, "Isn't that right, Mira?"

He called me Ino, the name of his dead sister.

"Ino knows I'm right," he said. Then closing his eyes once more, he added, "Kite zetwal yo tonbe." Let the stars fall.

His words evoked a loud wail from Tante Denise, who grabbed us by the hands and pulled us away from the bed.

"He's gone," she wailed. "My husband's dying. He's only speaking to people who aren't here."

The fact that my uncle had asked the stars to fall was also not lost on Tante Denise, who believed, and had groomed us to accept, that each time a star fell out of the sky, it meant someone had died.

I wasn't looking at the sky when my uncle died at Jackson Memorial Hospital, but maybe somewhere a star did fall down for him.

Thinking, as Pratt had been told, that my uncle was only being tested and observed, I spent the day waiting for his discharge and release. But late in the afternoon, I had a terrible feeling and began to frantically call the hospital until I reached a nurse in Ward D, the hospital's prison ward.

My uncle was resting, she said, but she couldn't allow me to speak to him since any contact with the prisoners, either by phone or in person, had to be arranged through their jailers, in my uncle's case, through Krome. While Pratt pleaded with the higher-ups at Krome to let us visit, I pleaded with the nurse to let me speak to my uncle. But neither one of us got anywhere, not even after my uncle died.

When a close friend of Maxo's, whom Maxo had used his one allowable phone call from Krome to tell, telephoned to break the news to me, I called Ward D again to ask if indeed it was true that a Haitian man named Joseph Dantica had just died there. The man who answered curtly told me, "Call Krome." And when I did telephone Krome—thinking I should have an official answer before calling my relatives—I was told by another stranger that I should try back in the morning.

By then it was nearly midnight.

"Don't tell your family now," my husband said, rocking me as I sobbed in his arms. "At least let them get *this* good night sleep."

We spent most of the night awake, cradling along with my large belly this horrendous news that those who most loved my uncle were not yet aware of. Some, like my father, were probably still praying for his release and recovery. Others, like his sisters in Haiti, were surely worrying, dreading perhaps, yet never expecting this particularly heartbreaking ending.

Waiting for daybreak, we reorganized the room in which my uncle was to have stayed, removing the paintings from the walls and stripping the bed of the sheets he was supposed to have slept on. As we slid the bed from one side of the room to the other, I worried for my father. Would he survive the shock? Placing a new set of curtains on the windows, after my husband had collapsed into bed, I worried for my daughter too. How would this stress, my sleeping so little, my lifting and lowering things and stooping in and out of closets in the middle of such a painful night affect her?

The next morning, my first call was to Karl, who conferenced the rest of the calls with me. We called Uncle Franck, who moaned loudly over the phone, then my mother, who, as always, was the most composed.

It was best that she, Bob and Karl tell my father in person, she said.

My father was in bed, weakened but tranquil after yet another sleepless night, when they told him. For a moment he was absolutely still, then he pushed his head back and looked up at the ceiling and then again at my mother and brothers. He didn't say anything at all. Perhaps he was numb, in shock. He didn't appear surprised either, my mother said. It was, she said, as if he already knew.

Brother, I'll See You Soon

Though we had been concentrating most of our efforts on getting my uncle released before tackling what we expected to be Maxo's much more challenging case, Maxo was freed from Krome to bury his father. While calling some of my uncle's friends in Port-au-Prince to make funeral arrangements, he was told not to bring the body back to Haiti. News of my uncle's detention and death had already spread in Bel Air and the gangs had rejoiced, all the while vowing to do to my uncle in death what they'd been unable to in life, behead him.

"They don't want him back in Haiti," Man Jou shouted loudly over the phone. "Neither alive nor dead."

At the same time, Maxo was reluctant to bury his father here in the United States, where in the end he had been so brutally rejected. He also felt bound by his father's wish to have his remains in the family mausoleum, next to Tante Denise's.

Cremation was to me the obvious choice.

"When things are calmer," I told Maxo, "we can all go back and bury his ashes on his own soil with Tante Denise."

My uncle's religious beliefs wouldn't allow it, Maxo said.

"In the final day of judgment," he added, "when the dead rise out of their tombs, we want his body there."

In the final day of judgment, will my uncle care from whence he'd rise?

Uncle Joseph's most haunting childhood memory, and the only one he ever described to me in detail, was of the year 1933, when he was ten years old. The U.S. occupation of Haiti was nearing its final days. Fearing that he might at last be captured by the Americans to work in the labor camps formed to build bridges and roads, my grandfather, Granpè Nozial, ordered him never to go down the mountain, away from Beauséjour. Uncle Joseph wasn't even to accompany his mother, Granmè Lorvana, to the marketplace, so that he might never lay eyes on occupying marines or they him.

When he left home to fight, Granpè Nozial never told my uncle and his sisters, Tante Ino and Tante Tina, where he was going. (The other siblings, including my father, were not born yet.) Granmè Lorvana told them, however, that their father was fighting somewhere, in another part of the country. She also told them that the Americans had the power to change themselves into the legendary three-legged horse Galipòt, who, as he trotted on his three legs, made the same sound as the marching, booted soldiers. Galipòt was also known to mistake children for his fourth leg, chase them down and take them away.

Still, my uncle and his sisters were never to let on that they knew anything about their father's whereabouts. If they were ever asked by an adult where Granpè Nozial was, they were supposed to say that he had died, bewildering that adult and sending him/her directly to Granmè Lorvana to question her. But when Granpè Nozial returned from his trips, they were not to ask him any questions. Instead they were to act as though he'd never left, like he'd been with them all along. This is why they knew so little of Granpè Nozial's activities during the U.S. occupation. This is why I know so little now.

One day while Granpè Nozial was away and Tante Ino and Tante Tina became ill, Granmè Lorvana had no choice but to send my uncle to a marketplace down the mountain. As Uncle Joseph walked to the market, following the road that his mother had indicated, what he feared most was running into Granpè Nozial, who'd threatened him with all manner of bodily harm if he ever found him on the road leading out of Beauséjour.

When my uncle finally reached the marketplace at midday, after hours and hours of walking, he saw a group of young white men in dark high boots and khakis at its bamboo-fenced entrance. There were perhaps six or seven of them, and they seemed to be kicking something on the ground. My uncle had never seen white men before, and their pink, pale skins gave some credence to his mother's notion that white people had po lanvè, skins turned inside out, so that if they didn't wear heavy clothing, you might always be looking at their insides.

As my uncle approached the small circle of men and the larger crowd of vendors and shoppers watching with hands cradling their heads in shock, the white men seemed to him to be quite agitated. Were they laughing? Screaming in another language? They kept kicking the thing on the ground as though it were a soccer ball, bouncing it to one another with the rounded tips of their boots. Taking small careful steps to remain the same distance away as the other bystanders, my uncle finally saw what it was: a man's head.

The head was full of black peppercorn hair. Blood was dripping out of the severed neck, forming dusty dark red bubbles in the dirt. Suddenly my uncle realized why Granpè Nozial and Granmè Lorvana wanted him to stay home. Then, as now, the world outside Beauséjour was treacherous indeed.

Uncle Franck flew down from New York the next day to help with the funeral arrangements.

"Mira and I think he should be buried in New York," he said.

We were driving to a funeral home in North Miami, where my uncle's body had been transferred after an autopsy at the medical examiner's office. The medical examiner had determined that my uncle died from acute and chronic pancreatitis, which it turns out he'd never shown any symptoms of before he became ill at Krome and for which he was never screened, tested, diagnosed or treated while he was at Jackson Memorial Hospital.

The advantage of a New York funeral, Uncle Franck explained on the way to the Miami mortuary, was that my father might be able to attend. Besides, after visiting there for more than thirty years, my uncle had a lot of friends in Brooklyn. It was the next best thing to Port-au-Prince.

. . .

When we got to the funeral home, Maxo asked to see his father's body. The manager was reluctant to allow it, but Maxo insisted.

"I need to see him," he said. "I just need to see him."

"A lot of people think they want to view a body," the manager said, "but then they find it's too much, especially so soon after an autopsy."

"I don't care," Maxo said, sounding like a little boy pleading for a favor from an adult. "I want to see him."

"Okay, then." The manager gave in. He was a tall, slender, butterscotch-colored man wearing a pastel-colored shirt and tie. His jacket was resting on the back of his swivel chair and he'd pick up the jacket and put it on each time he got up, then would take it off when he sat down again.

"I'll let you see him," he said, grabbing his jacket, "but we can't bring you into the room where the other dead are. We must respect them. We must also ask you to speak in a moderate voice and not curse. Here we treat the dead with respect as though they were still alive."

He should have been at the airport with my uncle, I thought, or at Krome when the medic was twisting his neck and raising his head up and down, or at Jackson, where perhaps because he was a prisoner—an alien prisoner, a Haitian one at that—he received what most doctors to whom I and others have shown his file agree that, given his age and symptoms, was deplorable care.

"You shouldn't be part of this," the manager said, pointing to my belly. "You have a life in you. You have no place with the dead."

"But I'm going to the funeral," I said.

What I really wanted to say was that the dead and the new life were already linked, through my blood, through me. Still, I agreed not to view the body yet. Besides, the time to have seen my uncle would have been hours, days, weeks earlier, when it could have made a difference, when we could have both been comforted.

The body was brought out on a gurney to a room next to the manager's office. Maxo and Uncle Franck followed the manager into the room, leaving the door half open. Fighting the urge to peek inside, to see my uncle one more time, I sat with my back to the door. I thought of Granmè Melina peacefully slipping away in her sleep across the room from me when I was only a child, of Tante Denise lying naked on a metal table in the morgue on Rue de l'Enterrement, and I marveled at the relative ease of those situations. Surely there was nothing to fear. Of the many ways that death might transform the love that the living had experienced, one of them should not be fear.

I would have to look at my uncle immediately. How could I not? Turning around, I positioned myself to see him. He was covered from his legs up to his hips with what looked like blue tarp. His unshaven face had a thin layer of white cream, which the manager explained was supposed to keep the skin from retracting. There were squared marks with traces of glue spread out across his chest, most likely from adhesive electrocardiogram leads. After the autopsy, a line of gray rope had been used to sew the front of his body, from his neck down to where the blue tarp ended. His tracheotomy hole was sealed. His head was also sewn down the middle, from ear to ear, but with thinner, nearly transparent thread.

My uncle did not look resigned and serene like most of the dead I have seen. Perhaps it was because his lips were swollen to twice their usual size. He looked as though he'd been punched. He also appeared anxious and shocked, as though he were having a horrible nightmare.

When was he last conscious? I wondered. What were his final thoughts? When did he realize he was dying? Was he afraid? Did he think it ironic that he would soon be the dead prisoner of the same government that had been occupying his country when he was born? In essence he was entering and exiting the world under the same flag. Never really sovereign, as his father had dreamed, never really free. What would he think of being buried here? Would he forever, proverbially, turn in his grave?

My uncle looked even less like himself at his funeral in New York. Dressed in a brand-new tuxedo, he had so much eggplant-colored makeup on his face that he looked like he was wearing an ill-fitting mask. But it was my father who inspired gasps when he entered the church he had attended for more than thirty years. Dragging an oxygen tank behind him, he was panting as he walked toward my uncle's coffin. He was skeletal, a stick figure. He hadn't been able to attend services for some time, and most of his friends, the ones who hadn't visited him at home, had not witnessed his gradual deterioration.

Standing before my uncle's coffin, my father tugged at the

oxygen tube in his nose. He was wobbly, sweating. My three brothers surrounded him, formed a half circle around him, ready to catch him from any angle should he fall.

Tapping my uncle's cheek, as if to stir him from a fainting spell, my father simply said, "Brother, the last time we spoke, you said you were leaving me with a heavy heart. This time I'm the one leaving you with a heavy heart. We may not see each other again on this earth, but I will see you soon."

My uncle was buried in a cemetery in Queens, New York. His grave sits by an open road, overlooking the streets of Cyprus Hills and the subway tracks above them. During his life, my uncle had clung to his home, determined not to be driven out. He had remained in Bel Air, in part because it was what he knew. But he had also hoped to do some good there. Now he would be exiled finally in death. He would become part of the soil of a country that had not wanted him. This haunted my father more than anything else.

"He shouldn't be here," my father said, tearful and breathlessly agitated, shortly before drifting off to sleep that night. "If our country were ever given a chance and allowed to be a country like any other, none of us would live or die here."

Transition

There's a stage in labor called transition, when the baby, preparing to separate from the mother, twists and turns to pass through the birth canal. I am sure there is a similar stage for exiting life, though it might be less definitive. Still, as I go into labor—thankfully with a risen placenta—each time I wish for an easy transition for my daughter and myself, I wish the same for my father.

Our midwife, Colleen, encouraged me to add some personal touches to the lavender labor room at the birthing center, so I brought two old photos of my mother and father. In his picture, my father is a handsome, serious-looking twenty-six years old. He's wearing a pale jacket, a high-collared shirt, a pencil-thin tie and tortoiseshell glasses. My mother in hers is wearing a checked blouse with a giant button on the front. Her hair is straightened and her round face framed by small, star-shaped drop earrings. When Colleen sees my mother's picture, she thinks my mother is me.

I looked at my parents' sepia-toned faces intermittently

during the sixteen hours that I walked, lay down, sat in a tub, on a ball, on the toilet, in constant agony. How could my mother have done this four times? I wondered.

My mother once briefly told me the story of my birth. I was nearly born in a pebbled courtyard, outside the maternity ward of Port-au-Prince's General Hospital. My father was out of the city for his work and my mother, fiercely independent, proud and alone, was one of nearly a dozen women who were doubled over and wailing in the yard. There were too many of them and not enough doctors. No one even examined them until their babies crowned.

During her four hours of active labor, my mother tried very hard not to wish death upon herself. She staggered in and out of consciousness until a doctor finally surfaced and rushed her into the delivery room.

When my daughter was born, her face blood-tinted, her eyelids swollen with tiny light pink patches that Colleen the midwife called angel kisses, her body coiled around itself as if to echo the tightness of her tiny fists, I instantly saw it as one of many separations to come. She was leaving my body and going into the world, where she would spend the rest of her life moving away from me.

Groggy and exhausted, I asked Colleen, "Is it normal for me to think this?"

"Maybe you're one of those women who enjoys being pregnant," she said.

It wasn't so much that I enjoyed being pregnant. I simply liked the fact that for a while my daughter and I had been inseparable.

Looking at her tiny face, her bow-shaped lips so red that

her father said she looked like she was wearing lipstick, I remembered a message a girlfriend had sent me when my first niece and nephew, Bob's daughter Nadira and Karl's son Ezekiel, were born.

"May you be a repozwa," she'd written, "a place where children can rest."

I needed to rest myself, but I also wanted to speak to my daughter, cradle her, sing to her, inhale her mixed blood and soap smell, watch her ever so slightly open her eyes and tighten her mouth as she tried to make sense of all the new sounds around her: my husband's laughter, my mother-in-law's comparisons with relatives both living and gone.

I thought she most resembled my mother and pointed at the picture to prove it. But I also saw traces of my father, who my mother says was too frightened to hold me and my brothers when we were babies, but who would later hold my brothers' children, laugh and sing to them. I grieved for Uncle Joseph and Tante Denise, who would never hold my daughter, and for my Haitian cousins, including Tante Zi's son Richard, who might never know her. Or maybe she would return one day, to Léogâne or to Bel Air, to declare in heavily accented words that they were her family.

She might be honored by their nods of acknowledgment, the way they'd be forced to consent, "Of course, of course, I see the resemblance. You do look like your great-grandmothers around the cheeks. You do have the high forehead of your grandfather's kin." And hopefully those cheeks and that calabash-shaped forehead would gain her entry.

Looking into my daughter's eyes, I thought of my mother, who had faced these first hours alone after I was born. She had been made no promises, been offered no guarantees that either she or I would even live past that night. If something had been ruptured inside of her, no one would have noticed. If something had been broken inside of newborn me, perhaps no one but my mother would have cared. My daughter's quiet yet well-monitored first night was perhaps the one my mother had dreamed for me, for herself, a dream of kind words, kisses, flowers.

"What have you decided to call her?" asked Colleen.

My husband and I had discussed it. There seemed no other possible choice.

"Mira," I said. "For my father."

After patiently waiting his turn to hold her, my husband held out his hand. I was also reluctant to let this Mira go. Hopefully I'll have an uninterrupted lifetime with her, I thought, a lifetime to plant some things that have been uprooted in me and uproot others that had been planted. But surrender her I did, with an urgent wish to also hand her over to my father.

Look, Papa, I'd say. You've waited for her. You've lived long enough to see her. Today is not just her day, but all of ours. And we're not the only ones who will cradle and protect her. She will also hold and comfort us. She too will be our repozwa, our sacred place to rest.

I said no such thing when we actually brought my daughter to meet my father three weeks later, five months after my uncle's death. Standing at his bedside, I was stunned by how motionless he seemed, how much he appeared to have aged. The room too was stripped of all signs of verve. The oak-framed queen-sized bed he once shared with my mother had now been replaced by a narrow hospital bed that allowed him to prop himself up at the push of a button.

My husband lowered the bed's railing and slipped our daughter into my father's scrawny arms. I thought that at nearly nine pounds, she might prove too heavy a weight for him, but he raised her face close to his and planted a kiss on her forehead. Her eyes were closed. She was sleeping.

"Do you know how long I've been waiting to meet you?" he said. "And you're not even awake."

A smile formed on my father's lips, which proved too much of a strain. He handed Mira back to my husband and began to cough.

After my husband returned to Miami, during the month that Mira and I would spend with my father, each time he held her, his smile would threaten to dissolve into a coughing spell and, after just a few minutes, I'd have to take her back. Until one morning when he'd walked out of bed by himself and over to the recliner by the window.

"Let me hold her," he said, "while you take a picture, for posterity."

I ran to my old bedroom and grabbed my camera. I had been hesitant to photograph Mira and my father during the brief moments he'd had her in his arms. I wanted him to enjoy those times as best he could without worrying about posing. Besides, as he'd grown sicker and thinner, he'd asked us not to photograph him. He wanted to be remembered, he said, the way he looked when he was well.

"Look at us, the two Miras," he said, staring into the camera. In the first frame, my daughter's eyes are half open, as though she's struggling to stay awake.

"I'm really touched that you named her Mira," he said, as I snapped another picture. "Now even when I'm gone—and we all can say that, even those of us who are not sick—even when I'm gone, the name will stay behind."

My daughter was now fast asleep. For the next shot, my father looked down at her and smiled, a smile that miraculously did not trigger his cough.

Later that week, we celebrated my parents' fortieth wedding anniversary, my brothers and I, our spouses and a few close friends, by gathering around my father's bed and toasting him and my mother.

My father was too weak to raise a glass of apple cider to his lips. Sweating profusely, he tried to say something, but couldn't. My mother quickly asked us to clear the room—he'd grown too hot—to give him some air.

Soon after we left the room, a friend of my father's from church told me, "Why don't you let him go? Tell him it's okay to go."

I couldn't, I told her, because I didn't want him to go. I didn't want him to die.

During the day, my father hardly ate anything. At night he couldn't sleep. Whenever he took a sleeping pill and dozed off for a few hours, he spoke loudly, incomprehensibly in rapid staccato speech. There were people, long dead, standing at his bedside, he would explain the next morning. His mother in a red dress. His father singing. His sister laughing. They were keeping him awake.

"Stay with me a while," he'd tell my mother and me, after he'd said his evening prayers. Then he'd dismiss us a half hour later, saying, "I suppose you have to go. You can't sit here all night."

We would go reluctantly, leaving our doors open so we could easily hear the slightest stir. He would get hot, then cold, in the middle of the night and call on us to open or close the windows.

Karl and Bob would come and bathe him, rub medicated lotions over the scaly patches of psoriasis on his skin, some as raw as open wounds. They would cut his hair, trim his curved, oxygen-deprived fingernails and toenails. I'd still watch his game shows and movies with him and, when he could, would debate the news from Haiti and elsewhere.

One afternoon, while my daughter was sleeping, I was sitting with him and my mother was downstairs in the kitchen, when he told me to ask her to cook him some plain long-grain white rice for supper. Early in his illness, he'd decided that rice grains were aggravating his cough, so he abruptly stopped eating them.

Overjoyed that he was actually craving food, I shared the news with my mother, who was downstairs cooking.

"Guess what?" I said. "Papa wants some rice."

My mother sent me back to ask exactly how he wanted his rice prepared. Could she soak it in chicken broth, mix it with black or brown beans or mushrooms, sprinkle it with shredded cashews? Would he mind if she lubricated it with butter or margarine to add some extra calories and taste, stirred in chunks of sausage or bacon for much-needed protein? Perhaps he wanted some fresh vegetables thrown in for fiber?

He only wanted a small bowl of the plainest white rice she could possibly prepare, he said. He even provided a shorthand recipe. "Cup of rice, water, drop of salt, spoonful of vegetable oil so nothing sticks to the pan. Boil it all."

My father had always been a picky eater. However, he had only learned to cook during his early years in the United States, while my mother was still in Haiti. When she joined him two years later, the first thing he did was cook for her.

My mother's first Brooklyn meal was very much like Bob's and mine. It consisted of stewed chicken, fried sweet plantains, which my mother loves, and diri ak pwa, rice and beans. For a while, each time someone would visit from Haiti, my father would help cook that same meal, just as he had for us, his welcome repast, he called it, because he wanted his visitors to taste something that had buffered his transition to immigrant life. And even if their stays were not meant to be as long as his, he hoped that they would feel, as he did, that one could easily return home, simply by lifting a fork to one's lips.

I watched as my mother prepared my father's rice. As she dropped the contents of an overflowing measuring cup into a pot of boiling water, a few grains spilled over the side, turning black in the burner's blue flames. Her hands trembled as she lowered the lid to trap some steam to prevent the rice from becoming sticky. My father liked his rice light and fluffy, but separate. If given the choice, he'd rather eat it al dente than soggy. Since he'd gone so long without a taste, the possibility of disappointing him weighed heavily on my mother.

When the rice was done, my mother searched a cabinet filled with her special-occasion dishes, the kind she used only when she had company, and pulled out a white porcelain plate with two giant cherries sketched in the middle. The cherries overlapped in a way that made them look like one large heart and as my mother heaped the rice on top of them, they seemed like a coded message from a woman who was beyond taking ordinary moments with her husband for granted.

I took the rice up to my father on the bright yellow tray on which all his meals were served. My mother added a tall glass of ice-cold water, which my father had requested at the last minute. When I walked into the room, my father's face lit up, his eyes sparkling with anticipation. He was sitting in the recliner, his eyes glued to the plate. I leaned over to place the tray in front of him. He was covered in four layers of blankets, which were doing the work that muscle and fat had once done for his body. What seemed like room temperature to someone else could feel glacial to my father.

The forward sway of my body made the water glass skid across the tray, spilling the chilled water into my father's lap. The water soaked through the blankets onto his pajamas, leaking into the sponge padding beneath him.

My father let out a loud cry. I quickly pulled the tray aside, resting it on the dresser behind the television. Even as he moaned and tried to wriggle away from the soaked sheets, my father's eyes trailed the plate of rice that was now cooling off just a few feet away.

My mother heard my father's screams from downstairs and rushed to his rescue. She quickly peeled back the blankets, all the while shouting for me to get her a towel and dry pajamas from the closet.

My father's pained utterances quickly went from moans to wails.

"Oh God!" he called out tearfully. "Oh God!"

An hour later, my father was still trembling, under no fewer than three piled-up dry comforters.

"It feels," he said, "as though I've been sleeping on a bed of ice for days."

It took some oxygen and a nebulizer to stabilize him. By then the rice was cold and he showed no desire for it.

'I'm sorry, Papa," I said, trembling myself at his bedside. I had terrible visions of watching him freeze to death as a result of my carelessness.

"It was an accident." He raised one bony hand from under the comforters to grab mine. "I know you didn't mean to do it."

"I am sorry I ruined the rice for you," I said. "I know how much you wanted it."

He hesitated, then pressed my hand harder.

"I didn't want it so much as I *wanted* to want it," he said. "The truth is, I don't feel hungry or thirsty anymore. I just wish I did."

It pained me much more to hear this than it did to have heard him say a few weeks before that he'd dreamed of

Granpè Nozial and Granmè Lorvana and Tante Ino, his long-dead father, mother and sister, standing at his bedside. It pained me more than the way he'd been starting every sentence with "Lè m ale." When I'm gone.

Sitting beside him that afternoon, I remembered being angry with him two Thanksgivings before when he'd sat down at the dinner table and left his plate untouched.

"There's nothing here I want to eat," he had declared.

After cooking for two days, my mother had been devastated by what she'd considered a blatant condemnation of her cooking. But what we didn't know then, and what my father himself wasn't aware of at the time, was that he already had a disease that was slowly eating away at his body, including his yearning for food and his reliance on it to sustain him.

We could smell it before we saw it. A new batch of long-grain white rice prepared by my mother. This time she brought it up herself and not on the bed tray, but on a round silver server from the special cabinet. My father raised himself on the bed to receive it and as soon as my mother handed him the spoon, for he always ate his rice with a spoon, he immediately dived in.

He barely chewed at all, simply bouncing the grains from cheek to cheek, then swallowing quickly. Had I not known, I would have thought him famished, ravenous, even insatiable. And perhaps he was. Or maybe he was desperately trying to nourish himself with something recognizable and familiar.

When he was halfway done, my father handed me the plate.

"Do you want some?" he asked.

"There's more in the kitchen," my mother said. "She can have some later. This is for you."

"Let her have some," he insisted.

I reached over and took the plate. Using my father's spoon, I piled a mound of rice into my mouth. It was plain but flavorful. I suspected that my mother had slipped in some broth or margarine, even a few drops of coconut milk.

I realized that afternoon that for nearly a year, while my mother, brothers and I had constantly carried food up to my father, we had rarely eaten *with* him. Somehow it hadn't occurred to me that he missed sharing a table or a plate, passing a spice or a spoon. But he did. Just as he missed seeing certain faces and places and hearing certain voices that neither his friends nor family nor the television could successfully transport to his room.

I returned to Miami with my daughter the next morning. Three days later, Bob called me before daybreak. I knew from the timing that it was not good news.

"He's gone, isn't he?" I asked.

"He's gone," he replied.

I think now that my father waited for me to leave. That he did not want me to hold Mira with one hand and his corpse with the other.

The night my father died, my mother heard the same type of rapid staccato speech coming from his room that she'd now grown accustomed to. In the middle of it, he somehow managed to shout her name. She ran into the room and found him sweating and gasping for breath. She made sure the oxygen tube was properly placed in his nose and tried to slip a nebulizer tube between his lips.

"M pa kapab," he told her. I can't.

His eyes rolled back in his head, which fell back, limp, against his pillow.

My mother called Bob, who came over and, after calling my father a few times ("Pop!") and after placing a nebulizer mask over his nose and mouth and getting no response, called 911.

When the paramedics arrived, they asked Bob if my father had a DNR. Bob said no. A clear measure of our inability to release him, we hadn't encouraged him to make one even after the doctor at Columbia Presbyterian had suggested it.

The paramedics removed my father's clothes, laid him on the wooden floor in his room naked and pounded at his chest for an hour. Even if they had succeeded in resuscitating him, he probably would have had a couple of broken ribs.

Neither Bob nor my mother could stay and watch, so as the paramedics worked on my father, they went downstairs, where they were interviewed by a policeman.

The policeman, the distant outside authority figure, was a curious presence. Was this standard practice in all American deaths, even expected ones like my father's? I asked my mother and brother.

It was, the policeman had explained, a measure to make sure there was no foul play, no euthanasia involved.

How long had my father been sick? the policeman asked my mother and brother. What medications was he taking?

When I was home with my father, just a few days before, lying with my daughter in the same bed I'd slept in as a teenager, there were nights when I stayed awake wondering what I'd do if I woke up the next morning and found my father dead. During those nights, heeding his friend's call to let him go, I would do a kind of mental rehearsal of several possibilities.

When it seemed irreversible and absolutely definite that my father was dying, I would finally tell him to go.

Don't be afraid, I'd say. It's okay. We love you. We will always remember you. Then naming each of us, I would tell him that we'd be fine and so would he. Manman will be fine, I'd say. Kelly will be fine. Karl will be fine. Karl's son Ezekiel will be fine. His daughter Zora will be fine. Bob will be fine. And his daughter Nadira will be fine. I will be fine and Mira will be fine. Then I would lean down and kiss him good-bye.

I don't know that I would have been able to do this. Perhaps the desire to see him return, to have him back, even for one more day, would have continued to be too strong.

Granmè Melina once told a story about a daughter whose father had died. The daughter loved her father so much that her heart was shattered into a hundred pieces. When it came time to plan for the jubilant country wake, which was once held the night before all funerals, the daughter wanted no part of it and ordered that it not be held.

"Daughter," said one of the wise old women in the daughter's village, "let the people rejoice at your father's wake tonight before they cry at his funeral tomorrow."

"There will be no rejoicing," answered the daughter. "Why should I ever rejoice again when my father is dead?"

"Daughter," insisted the old woman, "let the wake be held. Your father is now in the land beneath the waters. It is not our way to let our grief silence us."

Knowing that the old woman had the gift that the ancestors granted to only a chosen few, of being able to journey between the living and the dead, the daughter said to the old woman, "I will allow the wake to be held only if you go to the land beneath the waters and bring my father back."

The old woman walked to the nearest river and slipped into the waters. A few hours later, she reemerged and walked straight to the daughter's house.

"Where's my father?" asked the daughter.

"Daughter," said the old woman, "I am back from beneath the waters, deep into the bowels of the earth. There were some wide and narrow roads. I took them. There were many hills and mountains, and I climbed them. There were hamlets and villages, towns and cities, and I passed through them too. And finally I reached the land of the ancestors, the city of the dead."

"Did you see my father?" asked the daughter impatiently.

"I saw so many people there I couldn't even tell you," answered the old woman. "I saw my mother and father, my uncle and grandmother, my aunt who was trampled by a horse and my sister who died of tuberculosis in childhood. All my loved ones who've died were there."

"Did you see my father?" shouted the daughter.

"Daughter," answered the old woman, "I looked and I looked amongst all those people until I found your father."

"Where is he?" asked the daughter.

" 'I've come to take you back to the land of the living,' I told your father. 'Your daughter's heart has broken into a hundred pieces and she cannot live without you.' "

"What did he say to that?" asked the daughter.

" 'I'm so touched that my daughter wants me to come back,' he said, 'but my home is now here, in the land of the ancestors. Tell my daughter for me that when one is alive, one is alive, but when one is dead, one is dead.' "

The old woman then pulled from her pocket a set of false teeth that the father had religiously worn in his mouth when he was still among the living and had taken with him into the land of the dead.

"Your father sent you this," said the old woman, "so that you might believe that I saw him and accept what he says."

The daughter took the false teeth in her hands and looked at them with great sadness, but also with a new sense of courage.

"As my father wishes, so it shall be," she said. "We will have the wake to honor him, to rejoice and celebrate his life before his body is put in the ground. We will eat. We will sing. We will dance and tell stories. But most importantly, we will speak of my father. For it is not our way to let our grief silence us."

A few months after my father died, my parents' house caught fire. The fire started at three a.m., in the same room where my father had lain in bed for nearly a year, in the corner where we once kept his emergency supply of several oxygen tanks. Given the nature of the fire—crackling in the walls, sparks in the ancient wiring, electricity—the fire marshal predicted that the entire house, which lost part of its roof and a few walls, could have been totally razed in fifteen minutes. Enough time, thankfully, for my mother, my brother Karl and his family, who'd moved in with my mother, to all quickly escape. But not enough time for my father, in the state he was in, to have gathered himself up and made his way out. He might not have even heard the hiss of spreading flames over the loud hum of his oxygen compressor, or seen the smoke beyond the ghostly faces that haunted his final nights.

After my uncle Joseph died, my father told me that he dreamed of him only once, and never in the small group he pictured around his bed. In my father's dream, when my uncle calls him from Maxo's apartment the night he nearly died, my father actually makes it there on time to ride in the ambulance with him and hold his hands as the paramedics drill the tracheotomy hole in his neck.

"He must have been so scared," my father said, "not knowing whether he was going to live or die."

Like perhaps most people whose loved ones have died, I wish that I had some guarantees about the afterlife. I wish I were absolutely certain that my father and uncle are now together in some tranquil and restful place, sharing endless walks and talks beyond what their too-few and too-short visits allowed. I wish I knew that they were offering enough comfort to one another to allow them both not to remember their distressing, even excruciating, last hours and days. I wish I could fully make sense of the fact that they're now sharing a gravesite and a tombstone in Queens, New York, after living apart for more than thirty years.

In any case, every now and then I try to imagine them on a walk through the mountains of Beauséjour. It's dawn, a dazzling morning over the green hills. The sun is slowly rising, burning through the fog. They're peacefully making their way down the zigzag trail that joins the villages to the rest of the world below. And in my imagining, whenever they lose track of one another, one or the other calls out in a voice that echoes throughout the hills, "Kote w ye frè m?" Brother, where are you?

And the other one quickly answers, "Mwen la. Right here, brother. I'm right here."

ACKNOWLEDGMENTS

I am extremely grateful to the Lannan Foundation for a crucial fellowship at a most crucial time. Thank you, Cheryl Little, Mary Gundrum, Sharon Ginter and the entire staff at the Florida Immigrant Advocacy Center for the acquisition, through legal action and extremely persistent Freedom of Information Act requests, of Krome, Jackson Memorial, Department of Homeland Security records and Office of the Inspector General reports so extremely crucial to this narrative. I am grateful to the Harvard Law Student Advocates for Human Rights and the Centro de Justiça Global in Rio de Janeiro and São Paulo, Brazil, for their March 2005 report *Keeping the Peace in Haiti? An Assessment of the United Nations Stabilization Mission in Haiti Using Compliance with Its Prescribed Mandate as a Barometer for Success*. Also to Irwin P. Stotzky of the University of Miami School of Law and Thomas M. Griffin, Esq., for their report *Haiti Human Rights Investigation: November 11–21, 2004*. Thanks to Representatives Kendrick B. Meek, Charles Rangel and Major Owens, Robert Miller, John Schelbe, Drew Hamill, Alix Cantave and Esther Olavarria for hearing us out. I am extremely grateful to Jonathan Demme, Joanne Howard, James and Stephanie McBride, Susan Benesh, Kathy Klarreich, Ira Kurzban, Leslie Casimir, Patrick Sylvain, Ron Howell, Patricia Benoit, Lewis Kornhauser, Daniel Wolff, Jim Defede, Gina Cheron, Tamara Thompson and Johnny

McCalla from the New York–based National Coalition for Haitian Rights for their interest and counsel early on. To John Patrick Pratt, for representing my uncle under extraordinarily difficult circumstances. For support and love shown to my father, I'd like to thank Elycin and Lourdes Pyram, Denifa Rejouis, Drs. P. Krishnan, Paul Farmer, Kethy Elysée, Jocelyn Celestin and Hearns Charles, Reverends Rene Etienne and Phylius Nicolas, Reverend and Mrs. Elima Maréus. Thank you, Nick, Maxo, Franck, Josephine and Zi Dantica, Nicole Aragi, Robin Desser, Alena Graedon, Bob, Kelly, Rose, Mia and Karl Danticat, Ruth and Garry Auguste, Issalia and Fedo Boyer. I would also like to thank Shari Daniels, Colleen Fogarty, Dahlia Porter, Carol Williams, Angela Bolivar, Maribel Lumus, Becky Sprouse, and the entire staff and students at the Miami Maternity Center, who helped with every moment of "catching" Mira.

Diane Wolkstein recounts a remarkable version of "The Angel of Death and Father God" as "Papa God and General Death" in her marvelous collection *The Magic Orange Tree and Other Haitian Folktales*. Harold Courlander does the same with "Who Is Older?" and "The Voyage Below the Water" in *The Piece of Fire and Other Haitian Tales*. Ruth Auguste's as yet unpublished memoir, *Mom in the Mirror*, tells Marie Micheline's story in greater and more exquisite detail.

ALSO BY EDWIDGE DANTICAT

THE DEW BREAKER

We meet him late in life: a quiet man, a good father and husband, a fixture in his Brooklyn neighborhood. As the book unfolds, moving seamlessly between Haiti in the 1960s and New York City today, we enter the lives of those around him and learn that he has also kept a vital, dangerous secret. Edwidge Danticat's brilliant exploration of the "dew breaker"—or torturer—is an unforgettable story of love, remorse, and hope; of personal and political rebellions; and of the compromises we make to move beyond the most intimate brushes with history.

Fiction/Literature/978-1-4000-3429-1

BREATH, EYES, MEMORY

At the age of twelve, Sophie Caco is sent from her impoverished village of Croix-des-Rosets to New York, to be reunited with a mother she barely remembers. There she discovers secrets that no child should ever know, and a legacy of shame that can be healed only when she returns to Haiti—to the women who first reared her. What ensues is a passionate journey through a landscape charged with the supernatural and scarred by political violence, in a novel that bears witness to the traditions, suffering, and wisdom of an entire people.

Fiction/Literature/978-0-375-70504-5

KRIK? KRAK!

When Haitians tell a story, they say "Krik?" and the eager listeners answer "Krak!" In *Krik? Krak!* Danticat establishes herself as the latest heir to that narrative tradition with nine stories that encompass both the cruelties and the high ideals of Haitian life. The result is a collection that outrages, saddens, and transports the reader with its sheer beauty.

Fiction/Literature/978-0-679-76657-5